Cathal Brugha

Cathal Brugha

FERGUS O'FARRELL

Published on behalf of
the Historical Association of Ireland
by

UNIVERSITY COLLEGE DUBLIN PRESS
Preas Choláiste Ollscoile Bhaile Átha Cliath
2018

First published 2018 on behalf of the
Historical Association of Ireland by
University College Dublin Press

ISBN 978-1-910820-27-8
ISSN 2009-1397

University College Dublin Press
UCD Humanities Institute, Room H103, Belfield,
Dublin 4, Ireland
www.ucdpress.ie

Cataloguing in Publication data available from the British Library

Typeset in Scotland in Ehrhardt by Ryan Shiels
Text design by Lyn Davies
Printed in Dublin on acid-free paper by
SPRINT-print

CONTENTS

Do mo thuistí agus Eilis Ní Fhearghail

*

FOREWORD

Originally conceived over a decade ago to place the lives of leading figures in Irish history against the background of new research on the problems and conditions of their times and modern assessments of their historical significance, the Historical Association of Ireland Life and Times series enjoyed remarkable popularity and success. A second series has now been planned in association with UCD Press in a new format and with fuller scholarly apparatus. Encouraged by the reception given to the earlier series, the volumes in the new series will be expressly designed to be of particular help to students preparing for the Leaving Certificate, for GCE Advanced Level and for undergraduate history courses as well as appealing to the happily insatiable appetite for new views of Irish history among the general public.

CIARAN BRADY
Historical Association of Ireland

ACKNOWLEDGEMENTS

First and foremost, I would like to express my deepest gratitude to my supervisor, Dr Conor Mulvagh, for all his work, assistance, encouragement and enthusiasm when I was writing my MA thesis in UCD in 2015. This book draws heavily on that work; if it has any merit, much of the credit must go to him. I would also like to thank Dr Regina Uí Chollatáin in the School of Irish, Celtic Studies, Irish Folklore and Linguistics in UCD for her help with this project. I am indebted to Ita Roddy who kindly sent on copies of her translation of Sceilg, *Cathal Brugha* (Dublin, 1942). Thanks also to Professor Cathal Brugha who spoke to me about Brugha's life and the possible location of sources. Rossa O'Briain kindly provided some source material. Séamus Helferty and Orna Somerville in UCD Archives were particularly helpful. Thanks also to Cillian Doyle and James Brady who provided me with countless books and many helpful suggestions throughout this project. I would also like to thank Eve Morrison, Turtle Bunbury, Tim Carey, Liz Gillis, Paul O'Brien, Mark Jenkins, Jack Morley, Robbie Byrne, Deirdre O'Farrell, Colm O'Farrell, Cillian O'Farrell, Barbara O'Kelly, Imelda McGran, Danny Morrison, Colm Glover, Anthony McIntyre, Stephen Kelly, Irial Glynn, Paul Rouse and Diarmaid Ferriter. All have helped me along the way. I would like to thank Ruth Hallinan, Conor Graham and Noelle Moran at UCD Press and Ciaran Brady for all their hard work and expertise in bringing this book to fruition.

Apart from my supervisor, three people in particular made great contributions to this project: Geraldine O'Farrell scrutinised the text and pointed out a multitude of mistakes and inconsistencies; Donal O'Farrell read and re-read many drafts as well as translating Irish documents, including Tomás Ó Dochartaigh, *Cathal Brugha:*

a shaol is a thréithe (1969); Eimear McGran read drafts, provided endless encouragement and listened to many hours of me talking about Brugha.

FERGUS O'FARRELL
July 2018

ABBREVIATIONS

BMH WS	Bureau of Military History Witness Statements
COS	Chief of Staff
DOIB	*Dictionary of Irish Biography*
GHQ	General Headquarters
II	*Irish Independent*
IMA	Irish Military Archives
IO	Intelligence officer
IRA	Irish Republican Army
IRB	Irish Republican Brotherhood
IV	Irish Volunteers
MSPC	Military Service Pension Collection
NLI	National Library of Ireland
UCDA	University College Dublin Archives
UKNA, WO	National Archives of The United Kingdom, War office
UVF	Ulster Volunteer Force

CHRONOLOGY OF BRUGHA'S LIFE
AND TIMES

1874
18 July Charles Burgess is born.

1899
Joins the Gaelic League.

1899
Changes name to Cathal Brugha.

1908
Joins IRB.

1909
Established Lalors candle-making company.

1910
Becomes President of the Keating Branch of the Gaelic League.

1912
8 Feb Marries Kathleen Kingston.

1914
26 July Takes part in Howth Gun-Running.

1916

24 April Easter Rising begins.

27 April Brugha badly wounded in fighting; taken to hospital but not expected to survive.

Autumn leaves hospital and quits the IRB.

1917

10 June Brugha and Count Plunkett arrested at Beresford Place and imprisoned for eight days.

25 October Brugha elected to Sinn Féin party executive at its convention.

27 October Brugha appointed Chairman of the Resident Executive of the Irish Volunteers.

1918

April Brugha goes to London to lead assassination mission.

Autumn Brugha returns to Ireland.

14 December General Election – Brugha becomes TD for Waterford.

1919

21 January First meeting of Dáil Éireann.

22 January Brugha elected acting president of Dáil.

1 April Brugha is succeeded by De Valera as President of the Dáil and becomes Minister for Defence.

1920

21 November Bloody Sunday.

1921

24 May Brugha retains seat as TD for Waterford – Tipperary East.

11 July Truce.

13 September Brugha suspends Richard Mulcahy.

6 December Treaty signed in London.

1922

7 *January* Brugha speaks against the Treaty during Treaty debates and attacks Collins.

16 *June* Brugha elected TD for Waterford – Tipperary East.

28 *June* The Four Courts are shelled by the Free State army; Brugha reports for duty in the Anti-Treaty IRA.

5 *July* Brugha mortally wounded outside Hammam Hotel.

7 *July* Brugha dies from his wounds in hospital.

Introduction

This is the first dedicated English-language biography of Cathal Brugha; two previous biographies in Irish have been published.[1] In 1947, he was treated to a third of a biography in English by J. J. O'Kelly (also known as Sceilg) in *A Trinity of Martyrs: Terence MacSwiney, Cathal Brugha, Austin Stack*.[2] All are hagiography. Brugha has escaped serious examination until now because of a lack of sources. He joined the secretive Irish Republican Brotherhood (IRB) in 1908 and from that time forward was involved in clandestine military planning against the British Empire. As Minister for Defence during the War of Independence, he lived in the shadows. The British knew almost nothing about him, referring to him in 1920 as 'the man with the quare name.' His secretive nature and covert lifestyle have meant that historians also know almost nothing about him. He kept no diary and destroyed virtually all correspondence. This book would not have been possible without the Bureau of Military History (BMH) Witness Statements. This archive was opened in 2003 and contains the testimony of 1,773 people who were involved in the independence project from 1913 to 1921. It is here for the first time that a fuller picture of Brugha emerges. More recently, these have been augmented by the Military Service Pension Files. These voluminous collections have allowed historians to construct a more rounded picture of the events of the Irish Revolution.

Diarmaid Ferriter has given a voice to sometimes forgotten people involved in the Revolution – women, children and the poor.[3] Roy Foster's mining of the diaries of the Revolutionary Generation has also given the elite a new voice in their own way. We are treated to their inner thoughts on a range of matters such as sex, violence, war and family.[4] The centenary decade (2012–22) has been a catalyst for a proliferation of publications. The O'Brien Press 16 Lives Series has put flesh on the bones of some of the forgotten names who were executed in the aftermath of the Rising.[5] Notwithstanding this, Brugha has remained neglected – until now.

Cathal Brugha was second in command at the South Dublin Union during the Easter Rising and served as Minister for Defence in the first two Dáils (1919–22). Despite his importance, Brugha receives only cursory mention in histories of the period. Typically, he is presented as honest, ignorant, stubborn, brave, devout, fastidious and cantankerous. He is viewed as a soldier, moulded in the physical-force tradition. He is cast as a resolutely committed republican, who was uninterested in politics and unconvinced of its effectiveness, harbouring a deep-seated hatred of Michael Collins, of whose fame he was jealous. Some say he did little work of substance in his role as Minister for Defence, others argue that he was diligent and effective. This generally negative image is compounded by the fact that no English-language biography of Brugha exists.

This book will challenge this one-sided depiction of Brugha as a solider rather than as a politician. Detailed analysis of Brugha reveals that he also possessed a conviction that Ireland must marry armed resistance with politics to win its freedom. Following the Rising, he left the IRB and, for the rest of his life, was opposed to the Brotherhood as he believed that such a secretive and conspiratorial cabal would be perilous for Irish democracy. As world leaders met in Paris following the end of the First World War, Brugha tried to prohibit attacks on the police as he believed it would impinge upon the Irish delegation's efforts to secure international recognition for the Republic at the peace conference. He was centrally involved in the inaugural meeting of the first Dáil, was elected 'President of the Ministry *pro tem*' and appointed a cabinet. Throughout the War of Independence, he strove to bring the Irish Republican Army (IRA) under the authority of the Dáil rather than leave it in the hands of unelected military men. These were the actions of a man who was convinced that politics had a central role to play in achieving Irish independence. This is not to say that he did not believe in violence: he fused politics and war together in pursuit of freedom.

Brugha has been cast as the arch-militarist. According to Michael Laffan, Brugha was 'an honest and courageous man with a strong but narrow mind, distrusted any form of compromise ... he felt more useful as well as more comfortable in the company of fellow soldiers than among politicians.'[6] Charles Townshend has written that he was 'happier with gun in hand, facing death, than he had been facing political disagreement in the council chamber.'[7] Michael Hopkinson has argued Brugha 'personified the survival of the unbending and intransigent Fenian tradition.'[8] But there was more to Brugha than this; this book will seek to challenge these assertions and demonstrate that Brugha saw violence and politics as being of equal importance in the struggle for independence.

The separatist movement was not a monolith. One of its great strengths was that it brought various strands of political opinion together under the broad banner of Sinn Féin. On the moderate side of the movement were figures like Arthur Griffith. A journalist and political theorist, he wanted to break the connection with England but he was never an ideological republican. He was active in areas of publicity and politics, but not warfare. As we move towards the centre, we meet Michael Collins and Richard Mulcahy. They, like Brugha, saw the need to use violence in tandem with politics to achieve Irish independence. Collins and Mulcahy fought in the Rising and emerged in its aftermath as important rebels. Collins straddled both sides of the independence movement with roles in the army, IRB and the government. Both men shared the same views on military policy, believing that a guerrilla war would be the most effective means of combating Crown forces. They endorsed the Anglo-Irish Treaty of 1921, with Collins arguing that it was a stepping stone which would lead Ireland to ultimate freedom at a later date. Given their acceptance of the Treaty, they are what might be regarded as *pragmatists* on the separatist spectrum.

Brugha and Éamon de Valera also operated in this middle ground, at least before the Treaty split. They were allies throughout the revolution. They shared the view that the IRA should operate as a traditional standing army instead of ambushing soldiers and disappearing back into the local community. Both had fought in the Rising, but later de Valera took on a more political role, while Brugha, like Collins, was both a solider and a politician.

After the Treaty split, the differences between Collins/Mulcahy and de Valera/Brugha looked starker than they were in truth. Ronan Fanning has convincingly argued that de Valera rejected the Treaty not because it was a compromise, but because it was not *his* compromise.[9] The alternative which he offered in Document No. 2 showed that neither he nor Brugha were 'doctrinaire Republicans.'[10] However, more extreme militarists began to shape events in early 1922. On the staunch militarist wing of the movement were men like Rory O'Connor and Liam Mellows. They were opposed to any settlement which fell short of a Republic. This group might be regarded as *the purists*. Brugha is often lumped in with this cabal, but to do so is to misplace him on the separatist spectrum. He opposed the purists on many occasions, arguing for unity with the pragmatists and speaking in favour of Document No. 2. For this, he was distrusted by Mellows et al. They viewed him as being corrupted by politics. During the last seven months of his life, Brugha became powerless to shape events as he had fallen between two stools: too purist for the pragmatists, too pragmatic for the purists. This book seeks to reposition Brugha on the spectrum of separatist opinion. It will attempt to demonstrate that he is much closer to the centre, alongside figures like Collins, Mulcahy and de Valera, than previously thought.

Collins and Brugha were at loggerheads long before the Treaty, though it drove a further wedge between them. Despite Brugha's stinging attack on Collins on the final day of the Treaty debates,[11] the two were close to each other in political terms right up to the start of the Civil War. Both sought to break the British connection by fusing politics and war. Both sought to find common ground with the opposing side in the aftermath of the Treaty split. Both were concerned with the drastic situation unfolding in the newly established Northern Ireland. They even spoke about setting aside their differences and leading a 'crusade' to defend embattled Catholics there in 1922. The animosity that festered between the two men grew out of a power struggle and personality clash. It was exacerbated by the fact that they ended up on opposing sides of the Treaty.

Collins is sometimes mistakenly viewed as a model constitutionalist, while Brugha is seen solely as an unbending militarist. It is especially easy to fall into this simplistic analysis if the Civil War is viewed as a conflict between democrats and autocrats. Historians such as John M. Regan have questioned Collins' commitment to democracy in the aftermath of the Treaty.[12] This book seeks to revaluate Brugha's role in the revolution. By examining his attitudes to violence as well as his inherent belief in politics, these two men may come to be seen as much closer to each other than is often assumed.

CHAPTER I

The Making of Cathal Brugha

Cathal Brugha was born Charles William St John Burgess and his descendants can be traced to County Carlow, where they appear to have settled around the town of Borris in the middle of the seventeenth century. Thomas Burgess, Cathal's father, was born in Dublin in 1827. In 1860, he married Maryanne, the daughter of a wealthy auctioneer. Thomas' father did not approve of the union, and Thomas was disinherited as a result. However, this did not inflict financial ruin upon the new newly married couple, as Maryanne inherited three houses: 12, 13 and 14 Great Charles Street, near Mountjoy Square. Thomas ran a successful antiques and furniture business from 6 Lower Ormonde Quay, the same street where his son would later set up his candle-making firm and where he also ran the Department of Defence from 1919–22.

In 1867, Thomas became involved with a furniture business in London and sold some of his Dublin interests to fund this new venture. By 1871, the year of the census, the family are listed as living in London along with their six children, Maryanne's two unmarried sisters and two servants. Thomas operated his furniture business from 72 Newman Street, close to Oxford Street. Disaster struck the family in March 1871 when a fire broke out in the furniture warehouse, destroying the property and its contents. The Burgesses would never fully recover from this blow, and it began a slide into financial difficulties. In 1881, Thomas was embroiled in bankruptcy proceedings in Dublin, and this led him to concentrate his efforts solely on his English business interests. In 1887 or 1888, Thomas chartered a ship packed with furniture to Melbourne and left it in the charge of his two eldest sons, Edward and Thomas. The venture was a total failure and resulted in the bankruptcy of the family. The two sons never returned to Ireland, and Thomas senior was forced to sell the family home at North Great Fredrick Street; the family moved to 13 Great Charles Street, one of the properties inherited by Maryanne from her father.

Charles Burgess was born in Dublin on 18 July, 1874. He was the tenth child of 14 siblings. The family lived on Richmond Avenue, just north of the city. Charles attended the Colmkille School on Dominick Street and moved from there to Belvedere College in 1888. He learned Irish at school, though he did not master it; this came later through his involvement in the Gaelic League. Primarily, the young Charles was a sportsman. Low-sized, but strong and dextrous, he excelled across a multitude of disciplines. His first biographer, Sceilg, in typical gushing style, described him as:

An amateur boxer, a splendid cricketer, powerful swimmer, resourceful footballer, promising hurler, second-best rope climber in 'the three kingdoms', first rate cyclist, dead shot and amongst the best all round athlete and gymnast in Ireland at the end of the last century.[1]

At the age of sixteen, Brugha swam the channel from Howth to Ireland's Eye through strong tidal currents. His brother Alfred recalled that whenever Cathal appeared on the pier at Howth and stripped off, a crowd would gather to watch him swim, such was his prowess.[2] In 1899, whilst on a cycling tour with Alfred and a cousin, the trio stopped into a pub. Here they met John Carrig, who introduced Charles to the Gaelic League, and so began his life-long association with the language revival movement.[3] The League had been established in 1893 by Douglas Hyde and Eoin MacNeill and was dedicated to preserving and promoting the Irish language and its literature. Initially a small organisation, membership surged at the close of the century, reaching 500,000 members across 600 branches by 1904. It was a social organisation that brought people together to learn Irish and attend dances and *feiseanna*, but it also served as a meeting ground for those with more radical political ideas. While the League was a non-political and non-sectarian organisation, it became an incubator for the developing ideas of separatism and independence.

Charles left Belvedere in 1890 and, according to Tomás Ó Dochartaigh, enrolled in a pre-medical course at Cecila Street where he obtained a 1.1 in his first year.[4] However, it seems that, due to his family's ongoing financial difficulties, he terminated his education and began working with Hayes and Finch, an English-owned company that dealt in religious goods. His new job saw him travelling around Ireland as a salesman. On these trips, he forged Gaelic League contacts throughout the country and spoke at many League events. He developed a reputation as a popular guest speaker and was always ready to assist other Craobhacha.[5]

BECOMING A REVOLUTIONARY: 1900–16

At the turn of the century, the 25-year-old Charles Burgess was living with his mother at Ardilaun Terrace in the north inner city, working as a travelling salesman and attending meetings of the Gaelic League. Over the course of the next decade, he was involved in the debate to make Irish a matriculation subject, spoke in favour of retaining Douglas Hyde as President of the League in 1908 and was elected President of the Keating Branch of the League – renowned for its espousal of the Munster dialect and the fluency of its members. It was during these years that he evolved from a language activist into a radical republican, and then eventually into a gun-runner and urban warfare commander. There was no single event that transformed Charles Burgess; rather, he evolved over time to become Cathal Brugha.

The most overt sign of this transformation was his decision to Gaelicise his name. In 1908, after various experiments with different Irish versions, he eventually settled on the name we are familiar with. He also stopped playing what were regarded as English sports and concentrated solely on Gaelic games. However, the most potent expression of Brugha's transition from a language activist to radical republican was his joining of the Irish Republican Brotherhood in 1908. Many later revolutionaries would also tread this path, graduating from Gaelic revivalists to violent insurrectionists.

The IRB was a secretive revolutionary organisation established in 1858 with the aim of achieving an Irish Republic through force of arms. Militarily active in the second half of the 1860s, they organised an abortive uprising in the Dublin mountains, invaded Canada with several hundred men and shot a policeman during an attempted rescue of their captured comrades in Manchester. They also carried out a dynamiting campaign on the British mainland in the 1880s. After decades of activity, with the membership growing old and torpid, the movement sank into decline until the veteran Tom Clarke returned to Ireland from America in 1907 and rejuvenated the ailing Brotherhood. Clarke had spent 15 years in British gaols for his part in the 1883 campaign and suffered under very harsh conditions. Neither sleep deprivation nor hard labour broke his indomitable spirit and he began instigating plans for revolution from his tobacconist shop on Great Britain Street in 1908. The IRB successfully infiltrated larger nationalist organisations such as the Gaelic League, the Irish Volunteers and the Gaelic Athletic

Association (GAA). They would use their influence in these bodies, most successfully in the case of the Volunteers, to further their own aim of violent revolution against Britain.

It was also during this time that Brugha established Lalors Ltd, a candle-making business, in partnership with the Lalor brothers who were Brugha's colleagues from Hayes and Finch. The brothers brought the financial backing of their father and so it was named after them. This proved to be fortuitous for Brugha, as, had the firm been in his name, it surely would have been the focus of much unwanted British attention during the War of Independence. According to Ó Dochartaigh,[6] Brugha broke from Hayes and Finch as he could no longer reconcile himself with working for an English company. He worked at Lalors until his death in 1922, running the Department of Defence from its offices on the North Quays.

Brugha was no political theorist. We do not know what books he read and he left no record of his thoughts on political systems. However, it is clear that he wanted to break Ireland's connection with England. This found easy expression in the 'republicanism' of the era. His mind was more attune to matters of business and industry, and this also informed the little we do know of his wider political outlook. He wanted to see native Irish companies replace English owned ones in Ireland.

Brugha remained an active Gaelic League member during this busy period, though he now also incorporated IRB business into his travels around the country. On one visit to Kilrush, County Clare, accompanied by fellow Keating Branch member Seán Mac Diarmada, he established an IRB circle in the area. Mac Diarmada was Clarke's protégé: a swarthy Leitrim man, he worked with Clarke, Bulmer Hobson and Denis McCullough to revitalise the Brotherhood. Brugha's inclusion in such IRB activity – establishing cells around the country – indicates that he was a trusted radical even at this early stage.

Though travelling, radical politics, League meetings and business concerns all drew heavily on his time, Brugha also managed to get married during this busy period. While attending an Irish class in Birr, County Offaly, in 1908, he met Kathleen Kingston. The two were married in Dublin in the summer of 1912.[7] The newlywed couple lived in Rathmines, a short walk south of the city centre, and while some republicans did live in the area, the neighbourhood was generally of a sturdy unionist disposition as one contemporary has memorably recalled:

The Rathminesian was terrifically, indeed embarrassingly loyal to the King and Empire, on certain aspects of which, its army and navy, for example, and its world-wide conquests, he was intensely interested and extremely well-informed. After that, his big interest was the delectable 'loyal burgh' of Rathmines. As for Ireland, for the greater part of it at all events, his interest was nil. And, indeed, as I am determined to make this narrative as candid as possible, I must say this for the Rathminsian: when his much vaunted loyalty was put to the great test in World War I, he was certainly not found wanting, but joined up at once in the Dublin Fusiliers, and in nine cases out of ten, never saw his beloved Rathmines again.[8]

Between 1900 and 1912, Brugha worked tirelessly for the various organisations with which he was involved: the IRB, Gaelic League and his business. However, external political events were unfolding which would transform his life and times.

ULSTER

Ireland had been lurching towards a showdown between unionists and nationalists since the introduction of the first Home Rule bill of 1886. Unionists took some solace in the fact that the House of

Lords had a conservative majority of hereditary peers and so were highly unlikely to ever pass the bill. However, when the Lords took the unprecedented step of rejecting the 'people's budget' of 1909, the Liberal Government moved to curtail their powers. The resulting Parliament Act of 1911 abolished the Lords' veto: they could now only delay bills for two years. This meant that Home Rule could no longer be vetoed in the Lords, and it was introduced in 1912 as a new bill. While unionists had always been implacably opposed to the introduction of Home Rule, these new constitutional arrangements added urgency to their opposition.

The Ulster Volunteer Force (UVF) was formed in January 1913 with the aim of keeping Ulster out of a Home Rule Ireland, by force if necessary. It grew quickly, and, by March 1914, it had 84,540 members.[9] Retired British army officers came to train and advise the force and they began importing arms. Prominent conservative figures such as Andrew Bonar Law, Henry Wilson and Hubert Kitchener did not condemn the force, though Liberal Prime Minster H. H. Asquith accused this cohort of being 'a complete grammar of anarchy.'[10] In September, James Craig and Edward Carson began 'to frame and submit a Constitution for a Provisional Government for Ulster.'[11] Civil war seemed imminent if Home Rule were passed. Then, in March 1914, Army officers stationed at the Curragh threatened to resign their commissions rather than enforce Home Rule in the north-east. This contributed to nationalist misgivings that the British government could not be relied upon to introduce Home Rule for the whole of the island. As F. X. Martin has asserted, 'not since the "Glorious Revolution" of 1688 had the army displayed this mutinous mood, and it was an ominous reminder that Ulster Protestants had played their part in overthrowing the English government of that time.'[12]

Alarmed by the growing militarism in Ireland, the government banned the importation of arms into the country on 4 December

1913. However, the UVF, buttressed by their alliance with powerful members of the opposition and rich with donations from wealthy benefactors, were not cowed by the new law. On the evening of 24–5 April 1914, 25,000 German rifles and 3,000,000 rounds of ammunition were landed at Larne, County Antrim.[13] There now existed in Ulster a well-armed paramilitary force, determined to keep the north east out of whatever Home Rule arrangement Britain intended to impose on the rest of the country. Ronan Fanning has convincingly argued that these events comprise 'the most successful of bloodless revolutions: the threat of force, sustained and carefully coordinated, sufficed to achieve the Unionist revolution.'[14]

NATIONALISTS

Nationalists took note of these developments in the north; their hopes were tied to John Redmond and his promise of Home Rule. However, with Ulster so steadfastly and provocatively opposed to its introduction, Home Rule for all of Ireland was in trouble. Writing in May of 1912 in *Irish Freedom*, the paper of the IRB, a Sinn Féin businessman known as The O'Rahilly recounted the political and military aspects of the 1798 rebellion. He proclaimed that 'in the last analysis the foundation on which all government rests is the possession of arms and the ability to use them.'[15] In the June issue, he encouraged the acquisition of arms once again: '. . . there are no disarming acts now. Rifles can be bought by anyone who has the price of them. Powder, while somewhat dearer, is as easy to obtain as sugar. Yet will anyone assert that Irishmen who desire a change of Government are armed to-day?'[16] This call to arms largely fell on deaf ears; the opportunity was not yet ripe for the arming of nationalists. In any case, there was not even an organised body of men to arm, but the sentiments expressed by

The O'Rahilly were indicative of the rising mood of militancy in Ireland, and indeed Europe. As Martin has pointed out, 'even the pacifist Francis Sheehy Skeffington and the moderate Douglas Hyde were so carried away by the militant wave sweeping through Ireland during 1913–14 to lend their voices temporarily to the chorus advocating the use of physical force.'[17]

In 1913, The O'Rahilly took over as editor and rejuvenated the stale Gaelic League newspaper, *An Claidheamh Soluis*. He approached the well-known northern academic Eoin MacNeill and asked him to write a leading article, which appeared on 1 November, 1913. The piece, entitled 'The North Began', spurred nationalist Ireland into action. MacNeill pointed out the dangers that the UVF posed to the Home Rule movement and called for the formation of a body of Irish Volunteers, ten times larger than Carson's force, in the 28 other counties of Ireland.[18] Things moved quickly and the inaugural meeting of the Irish Volunteers was held in Dublin on 25 November, 1913. The provisional committee was comprised of nationalists of all hues: IRB men like Éamonn Ceannt, Irish Parliamentary Party (IPP) MPs like Tom Kettle, and Sinn Féiners like The O'Rahilly.[19] Brugha was elected First Lieutenant of C Company of the 4th Dublin Battalion of the Irish Volunteers in November 1913 and, by the following spring, was Battalion Adjutant. Now that an organised body of men existed, The O'Rahilly's call to arms could be answered.

While the British had failed to move against the UVF, they were suddenly alarmed by the formation of the Irish Volunteers: in response, they banned the importation of arms into the country. The UVF, who had been either threatening or ignoring the government since at least 1912, defiantly imported their own shipment of arms in April 1914, contravening the government ban. Just as the foundation of the Irish Volunteers had been a reactionary response to developments in Ulster, the Larne incident would prompt the Irish Volunteers into acquiring their own weapons.

HOWTH GUN-RUNNING

The Volunteers formed an armaments subcommittee, and, through the help of Darrell Figgis and the acclaimed humanitarian Sir Roger Casement, they purchased 1,500 German Mauser rifles, relics of the Paris Commune. They were transported to Ireland by a yacht skippered by Erskine Childers, the former British civil servant turned sailor and espionage novelist. The Irish Volunteers' secretary, Bulmer Hobson, liaised with the gun-runners and organised preparations for landing the weapons in Dublin. Hobson was a northern Quaker, a member of the Gaelic League, and had been a founder of the Ulster Literary Theatre.[20] Most importantly, he was on the supreme council of the IRB and he proved to be an important nexus between these two organisations. The IRB were not involved in the planning of the Howth gun-running, but some of its key members were involved in the operation, including Brugha, Clarke and MacDiarmada.[21] Hobson was initially dismayed by the small quantity of arms that were to be landed, though these misgivings were later assuaged by the massive publicity that would be garnered by defiantly landing the guns in broad daylight. As Hobson recalled later, 'I decided to land the guns during daylight, in the most open manner and as near to Dublin as possible.'[22]

Hobson's planning was meticulous. He cycled from Greystones to Balbriggan, surveying every harbour, eventually settling on Howth – a small fishing village, nine miles north of the city. In an effort to counteract British suspicion of a large body of Volunteers marching out of the city on a Sunday morning, he ordered several route marches on the Sunday mornings in the weeks prior to the landing. The result was that the British soon lost interest in the parading volunteers. By 26 July, the day of the landing, the British considered 800 Volunteers marching out of Fairview unremarkable. Another potential snag was averted when Hobson managed to divert the British gun boat that was guarding the mouth of Howth harbour by strategically leaking false information that guns were to be landed at Waterford that week.[23]

Brugha commanded a group of about 20 IRB operatives at Howth on the morning of 26 July 'with instructions to comport themselves about the harbour, hire boats and generally look as much like tourists as possible.'[24] Other IRB men came to Howth accompanied by ladies and had lunch in the hotel. Upon seeing Erskine Childer's yacht, the *Asgard*, they abandoned both ladies and lunch to help unload the cargo. Hobson himself marched in from Dublin with the Volunteers. 'Fortunately' he recalled, 'we reached Howth just as the yacht sailed into the harbour. When we got to the harbour we put a strong guard at the entrance.'[25] Childers arrived into the quay just as Brugha, who had swum the channel between the harbour and Ireland's Eye as a teenager, marched along the pier to meet the *Asgard*.[26]

Mary Spring Rice's diary testifies to the joy of the crew upon arriving at Howth. Once moored, a brief, excited scramble broke out: 'then Erskine stopped the delivery until he got hold of someone in command and some sort of order was restored.'[27] The cargo was rapidly unloaded by the Volunteers and Fianna Éireann, a type of boy scouts founded by Hobson in 1902. Much of it was whisked back to Dublin by IRB men in taxis, but Hobson still wanted the spectacle of marching men armed with weapons to be a memorable part of the day. This was a provocative gesture, though he did take precautions. He would not allow any man load his rifle, as he was nervous of the untrained Volunteers discharging rounds in the event of trouble. As a column of men were marching back into the city, they were confronted by the army. As a Volunteer explained, the men were intercepted by the military while carrying the rifles on their shoulders.

> Some of the Volunteers went back towards Howth and Lieut. George Walsh went with them. As soon as this happened, 2/Lieut. C. Brugha ran up to the front of the remaining element of the Company that stood their ground and took over command. We got orders to line across the road, two deep, and we obeyed. Dan McCarthy and myself were in the front line, side by side. The military at this point were right up against us with fixed bayonets. The barricade that we drew up prevented the military from advancing and gave the volunteers at the rere [*sic*] an opportunity for getting their arms into safety. This opportunity was availed of to the fullest extent.[28]

The Howth gun-running was a logistical and propaganda victory for the Volunteers. The army fired on civilians at Bachelor's Walk later that evening, killing three people, with a fourth later dying of injuries. This, along with the confrontation with the Volunteers as they journeyed into Dublin, differed starkly from the government's refusal to act against the UVF's gun-running at Larne. A week later, the IRB landed more weapons at Kilcoole, County Wicklow. Once again, Brugha was actively involved.

Ireland was armed. As the two volunteer forces marched and drilled in their respective heartlands, the British government was becoming increasingly concerned that a civil war would break out. Their fears were only temporarily allayed by the assassination of the Archduke Franz Ferdinand in Sarajevo and the outbreak of war on the continent. Ironically, it was the beginning of the First

World War that averted bloodshed in Ireland, though many of the
prospective protagonists spilt their blood abroad, in the uniform
of the British army, rather than on home soil.

The Howth episode proved to be Brugha's public debut as a
radical. He acted coolly under pressure and was decisive in action.
He was always content to work in the shadows, but once the
prospect of fighting presented itself, he threw himself unreservedly
to the fore. This was to be a feature of his revolutionary career until
his death.

ENGLAND'S DIFFICULTY IS IRELAND'S OPPORTUNITY

John Redmond, the leader of the IPP, correctly saw the Volunteer
movement as an important new departure in Irish politics and so
moved to control it. Fearing a split, MacNeill acquiesced in allowing
Redmond's nominees onto the Volunteer's Provisional Committee.
But a split came nonetheless; Redmond's speech at Woodenbridge,
County Wicklow in September committed the Volunteers to the
British war effort and upwards of 90 per cent of the force enlisted
in the army. Off they went to Europe, leaving a small, more radical
9,000 Volunteers in Ireland.[29] Clarke and McDiarmaida, the IRB
infiltrators waiting in the wings, saw this as their chance to strike:
England's difficulty would be Ireland's opportunity. They intensified
their plans for rebellion. In the summer of 1915, they formed a military council, consisting of Clarke, McDiarmaida, Patrick Pearse,
Joseph Plunkett and Éamonn Ceannt.

By this stage, Brugha was a Battalion Adjutant in the Volunteers.
He continued his work as a commercial traveller around the
country and used these trips to carry out work for the Gaelic
League and the IRB outside Dublin. On Whit Sunday, 1915, he
travelled with the Dublin Brigade of the Volunteers to Limerick to
take part in a march, accompanied by Pearse and Clarke. The

march 'was marked by noisy scenes for which women were mainly responsible . . . At Mungret Street they were met by a fusillade of stones, jampots, bits of lead etc.'[30] These were the wives of men who were fighting for the British army in France and these protestations would be repeated almost a year later in Dublin in the aftermath of the Rising. One witness recalled the scene:

Prominent amongst the attackers on that Whit Sunday was a powerfully built amazon [*sic*], who seemed to have inherited in ample measure, the fighting characteristics of the women of Limerick, even if she was lacking somewhat in the more engaging feminine qualities. Where the disturbance was fiercest, this indomitable female, like a modern heroine of Ross – if not in so good a cause, nor in so worthy a manner – her hair flying, and her apron full of missiles, frenziedly rallied the mob to renewed excesses of stonethrowing, varied by attempts to snatch the rifles from the parading Volunteers.[31]

Undeterred by this obvious hostility, the military council continued plotting for rebellion. While Brugha was not centrally involved in the planning of the Easter Rising, he was certainly an active and trusted radical. He helped move guns and ammunition around the city by motorcycle at night, depositing them in sympathetic households (including his own) until such time as they were deemed necessary.[32] Though not on the military council, he was briefed on the plans in the event of any of the leaders being captured. The plans gestated through the autumn, drawn up by the dreamy Joseph Plunkett at his home in Larkfield, County Dublin, and guided by the veteran Clarke.

Brugha and his battalion continued to train.[33] The Volunteers were planning to assemble on Easter Sunday for manoeuvres. They would then be informed by the IRB members that the Rising was going to start. However, the Volunteer Commander, Eoin

MacNeill, was not as bellicose as his secretive IRB colleagues. He, along with Hobson, did not want to engage the British in an offensive war unless they were sure that the Volunteers were at risk of being suppressed. They also wanted to be sure of overseas aid from Germany. The military council kept the two of them in the dark. In early April, Brugha travelled to Kilkenny to liaise with the local IRB and finalise plans.[34]

<h2>THE RISING</h2>

As Easter approached, MacNeill and Hobson became suspicious. On Spy Wednesday, MacNeill was deceived by 'the castle document' which purported that the Volunteer leadership were to be arrested imminently. While the veracity of the document is debatable, it was certainly embellished by Plunkett with the aim of neutralising MacNeill's opposition to the Rising.[35] When it was thought that Bulmer Hobson might betray the rebels' plans to MacNeill, he was captured by the IRB on Good Friday and held captive at a house in Cabra.

Disasters struck thick and fast as Easter approached: an expected German arms shipment was scuttled off the south-west coast and the British became aware of the rebels' intentions but decided to postpone their reaction until after the Easter holiday. Roger Casement was arrested on a beach in Kerry, and MacNeill, recognising the Rising's doomed prospects, issued a countermanding order to the Volunteers, cancelling Sunday's planned assembly. The Rising now had no chance of success. Learning of the development late that night, a furious Brugha confronted MacNeill. He then called at the house of his commanding officer, Éamonn Ceantt, in the early hours to inform him of the situation.[36]

The leaders regrouped on Sunday and committed to push ahead with the Rising the next day, Monday, 24 April, despite the litany of mishaps. The British, meanwhile, were lulled into a false sense of security, believing that the arrest of Casement and the loss of the German shipment had scuppered the rebellion; with such little chance of success, they assumed that the Rising had been aborted.

On Easter Monday morning, Brugha left his pregnant wife and three children and set out to take on the British Empire. He was armed with a German Mauser pistol with a foldable wooden rifle butt attached by a hinge. It was known colloquially as a 'Peter the Painter' after the mythical Polish anarchist who was reputed to have been involved in the siege of Sidney Street in London's East End in 1911. It would be Brugha's favoured weapon over the next few years. The 4th Battalion of the Dublin Brigade of the Volunteers assembled at Emerald Square, Dolphin's Barn, and marched to the South Dublin Union under the command of Ceannt, one of the seven signatories of the Proclamation, which had been read aloud by Pearse outside the GPO that morning. The Union was 'the country's biggest poorhouse, with 3,000 destitute inmates, its own churches, stores, refectories, and two hospitals with full medical staff.'[37] Turnout was poor owing to the countermanding order,[38] with only about 120 of the nominal 700 men of the battalion reporting for duty.[39] The Volunteers occupied several buildings on the site, erected defensive barricades and broke holes through walls to link their positions. Through the main gate came a horse and cart laden with barbed wire, shovels and homemade hand grenades, manufactured at Plunkett's Larkfield military camp. The cart was then overturned and used to barricade the gate.

Brugha, who was second in command of the Battalion, posted men at defensive positions and awaited a British response. They did not have to wait long. A column of troops from Richmond barracks soon appeared and Brugha gave the order to open fire. Fighting continued throughout the day and the maze of rooms around the site turned the battle into a 'deadly game of hide and seek.'[40] Tuesday and Wednesday were quieter than Monday, but the most intensive fighting was yet to come. Each evening, Ceannt and Brugha gathered the men together and gave a summation of what had happened during that day's fighting. They then recited the rosary before retiring to rest. Many combatants inside the Union remarked on Brugha's piety during the week. One recalled that Brugha 'seemed the most silent member of the garrison. I noticed him most as he sat at the open back door of the home cleaning his automatic pistol, which had a wooden holster which also served as a shoulder butt, like a rifle. Brugha spoke (when he did) quietly, and always appeared composed and contented.'[41]

On Thursday morning, Ceannt and Brugha inspected the barricades and assessed their defensive position. With the Volunteers numbering only 41 officers and men, the British began a violent assault in the afternoon. Advancing under covering fire, members of the Royal Irish Rifles and Royal Munster Fusiliers stormed the buildings of the Union, eventually reaching the Nurse's Home, which served as the Volunteer HQ. A British officer, Major Vane, described the chaos in a letter to his wife:

> Well I have been in some fights but never in such an odd one as this, for we commenced by open fighting in fields and so far as right flank was concerned fought up to literally three feet of the enemy. But everything was bizarre on that day for we advanced through a convent where nuns were all praying and expecting to be shot poor creatures, then through the wards of imbeciles shrieking – and through one of poor old people. To get from one door to another was a gymnastic feat because you had to run the gauntlet of the snipers.[42]

At 3:30 p.m., the British battered the HQ with machine gun-fire as they tried to force their way in. Lumps of plaster fell from the ceiling as the rooms were filled with dust and smoke. Seeing a burly policeman attempt to breach the door, Ceannt and another volunteer forced it closed. Ceannt fired his pistol through a gap and shot the intruder. Above them on the second floor, Brugha fired down on the British from a window. The attackers eventually gained entry to the Nurse's Home by tunnelling though a wall, and fierce fighting followed. As the historian of the battle has written, 'the Volunteers hung tenaciously to their positions while Brugha urged them on. Walking between the rooms and the landing he continuously risked his life with the casual abandon of those who think they are invincible.'[43]

Amidst the confusion and chaos, the Volunteers began to retreat. Brugha became cut off from his men and, as he descended the stairs to the first floor landing, he walked straight into an exploding British grenade, ripping his short and sturdy body to pieces. The Volunteers regrouped in another part of the building and prepared for what they believed would be a final and fatal British assault. As they knelt for a decade of the rosary, the sound of Brugha's voice could be heard, goading the British to come out and face him: 'Come on you cowards, till I get one shot before I die. I am only a wounded man. Eamon, Eamon [sic], come here and sing "God Save Ireland" before I die.'[44] Ceannt led a rescue mission to relieve Brugha and found him 'sitting in the yard, his back resting against the outer wall, his "Peter the Painter" revolver to his shoulder, and waiting for the first move of the enemy to enter the building.'[45] Brugha was carried into a back room, where W. T. Cosgrave and Joe Doolan attempted to deal with his injuries. The British were eventually forced to retreat after some inexperienced recruits from the Sherwood Foresters fled in terror.

The fighting was so intense that Brugha's wounds could not be dressed until 7 or 8 p.m. This process took many hours, owing to the terrible injuries he had sustained. It was reported to Ceannt

that Brugha had 25 wounds: '5 dangerous, 9 serious and 11 slight . . .
His left foot, hip and leg were practically one mess of wounds.'[46]
He lost a huge amount of blood and became delirious during the
night. On Friday morning, Brugha was stretchered to a medical
ward in the Union by a priest and thence to the Dublin Castle
hospital by British escort.

Meanwhile, in the South Dublin Union, the Volunteers refort-
ified their positions and prepared for another British assault.
However, across the river, the embattled rebel General Headquarters
(GHQ) in the GPO – the centre of the rebellion – was contem-
plating surrender. On Saturday, Pearse surrendered unconditionally
to General Lowe in order to prevent further loss of civilian life.
The South Dublin Union was the last garrison to surrender, a day
later, and only did so on the orders of GHQ.

Brugha is to be commended for his role in the Rising. He fought
with courage and proved to be an inspirational leader to the men
under his command. He held his nerve in the cauldron of close
quarter urban warfare, and, along with Ceannt, proved to be a
decisive commander. This is all the more impressive given that this
was his first experience of combat. His defiant challenge to the
enemy to come out and face him as he lay injured and propped up
by a wall is indicative of his character: this was just the first of
many occasions when Brugha resolutely looked death in the eye and
resigned himself to it. He was fearless, reckless – and even perhaps
suicidal – in the face of danger. The thought of surrender would
never have crossed his mind. Every fight was a fight to the finish.

As Brugha lay in hospital, the surrendered rebels were corralled,
first in the Rotunda, and then moved to Richmond Barracks. The
British picked out the leaders from among their ranks and sentenced them to death; any others were shipped off to internment
camps in England and Wales. A warrant was issued for Brugha's
arrest, but as he was incapacitated in hospital he was allowed to

remain there. His British doctors reckoned he would succumb to his wounds – this was neither the first nor the last British miscalculation of the Rising.

Éamonn Ceannt was among those who were sent to the firing squad. His final letter reveals that he shared Brugha's abhorrence of surrender.

> I leave for the guidance of the other revolutionaries who may tread the path which I have tread this advice: never to treat with the enemy, never to surrender to his mercy but to fight to a finish. I see nothing gained but grave disaster caused by the surrender which has marked the end of the Irish Insurrection of 1916.[47]

These words echoed in Brugha's ears for the rest of his revolutionary career.

CHAPTER 2

Recover, Regroup, Rebuild: April 1916–November 1917

Brugha was transferred to the Richmond Hospital and later George V Hospital where he remained until the autumn of 1916. Though bedridden, he began rebuilding the Volunteers.[1] Henry Murray recalled being summoned to Brugha's bedside where he was informed that efforts were already underway throughout the country to reorganise the Volunteers and that Murray was to cooperate with the officer in charge of the reorganisation of the Fourth Battalion. Recruiting was not to commence for the time being, and no action was to be taken against those who had not reported for duty on Easter Monday. Murray described Brugha as being in 'very good spirits and full of enthusiasm, for the work in hand; he never hinted at the discomfort and suffering which he had endured and he discussed the position and prospects with me in a cheerful, even boisterous manner.'[2] This was typical of Brugha's stoicism; he never fully recovered from the wounds he received during the Rising. He walked with a limp for the rest of his life and carried British shrapnel inside his body until his death; despite these afflictions, Brugha never complained of pain. On 23 August, his internment order was revoked and he left hospital soon after to continue the reorganisation of Irish resistance.[3]

LEAVING THE IRB

Around this time, Brugha also left the IRB. He regarded the Brotherhood as redundant after the Rising and he did not trust its cloak and dagger politics. One Bureau of Military Archives witness recalled that Brugha explained to him that the IRB was 'no longer necessary; we have now an open military organisation in the Volunteers and there is no necessity for a secret one, and if it continues to exist it will only create trouble and do harm because it will be a case of too many cooks spoiling the broth.'[4] Historian of the IRB, Leon Ó Bríon, has correctly asserted that 'Brugha was bitterly critical because the IRB membership had not participated in the Rising in force.'[5] Brugha was not the only IRB man to revoke membership following the Rising. According to Ó Bríon, Éamon de Valera, Seán T. O'Kelly, Ernest Blythe and Desmond FitzGerald all exited the Brotherhood.[6]

Brugha was also suspicious of the secretive, conspiratorial workings of the IRB. Seán Matthews, an IRB member based in Waterford, remembered Brugha visiting the county when he was convalescing in late 1916:

> I have a clear recollection of him telling me that he had left the IRB for good and all, as he could see no use for it. When I asked him his reasons, he replied: 'All that the IRB in Dublin wanted was to pull their caps over their eyes, pull up the collars of their coats and be shadowed by detectives. Brugha also said to me that the only two men who could keep that organisation free from graft and corruption were Tom Clarke and Seán McDermott, and they were dead'.[7]

One Volunteer recalled meeting Brugha in Limerick in the summer of 1917. He remembers Brugha becoming animated when talking about the IRB: 'striking the table with his fist, he said: "I don't care

if it is that last act of my life I will lead a crusade to destroy it."'[8]
This account seems extreme and is perhaps an embellishment,
others speak of Brugha's distrust of the IRB[9], but not of a desire to
eradicate it. Brugha's exit from the Brotherhood, along with
Michael Collins' rising status within it, certainly contributed to
tensions developing between the two men later. When he was
Minister for Defence, Brugha strove to subordinate the IRA to
the Dáil and to counter the IRB's influence in both politics and
the army.

REORGANISATION

The executions and deportations in the wake of the Rising
decimated the Volunteers, though it left Brugha as the most
important physical force separatist in Ireland. His pre-eminence
was recognised when he was elected to the provisional committee
of the Volunteers on 7 August 1916, despite the fact that he was
still in hospital.[10] The prison experience instilled an *esprit de corps*
among those who endured it. Brugha missed out on this, and this
marked him out from his fellow revolutionaries; he had spent the
time alone, recovering from his serious wounds in Dublin.[11]
Following his discharge, he continued rebuilding the Volunteers.
Gatherings were sometimes held in his home, 6 Fitzwilliam Terrace,
Upper Rathmines, where he spent much of the year recovering.
Sometimes he ventured out to meetings in the city. In December,
all internees were released, except those who had been court-
martialled. These returned men augmented the force Brugha was
reconstructing, as well as providing experience and enthusiasm. At
this time, he concentrated on the reorganisation of the Volunteers,
and had little to do with Sinn Féin. There are a number of possible
explanations for this.

Even by the end of 1916, Sinn Féin 'remained small and uninfluential, and in terms of its membership it bore no relationship to the mass movement of the same name which would emerge within a few months.'[12] In this sense, perhaps Brugha did not view the party as being an important vehicle for delivering Irish independence. Sinn Féin was still a dual monarchist party, meaning that it sought to achieve a compromise with the British, with the English monarch remaining the titular head of the country. Brugha, however, was a republican who wanted complete and total separation from Britain. Michael Laffan has argued that Brugha (as well as Collins) 'regarded Griffith's Sinn Féin with deep distrust.'[13] Whatever the reasons, Brugha concentrated on military rather than political organisation after the Rising. It is, however, too simplistic to portray this as a distrust of politics and a belief in the efficacy of violence alone.

Brugha became progressively more active during 1917, which can most probably be attributed to an improvement in his health. In the spring, he chaired a meeting of the Volunteers in Fleming's Hotel where they discussed the dire need for weapons.[14] On 21 May, de Valera and Brugha spoke at a rally at the Mansion House about the conditions faced by Irish prisoners in Britain. The *Irish Independent* reported that 'Cathal Brugha said that prison diet was now less in weight by 100oz. If Ireland accepted no bribe between now and the Peace Conference the day of her deliverance was at hand.'[15] Brugha, like many separatists, believed that the Irish republic would be recognised by world leaders meeting in Paris in the aftermath of the Great War, another reflection of his belief in the importance of politics.

While Brugha played an important role in the reorganisation of the Volunteers, this role should not be exaggerated. He contacted members from around the country and encouraged them to reorganise the movement in their own localities. However, the Volunteers had no resources at their disposal. A directive issued by the Executive on 22 May, 1917, acknowledged this. It stated that every Volunteer 'is expected to do his own part under the present difficult circumstances towards making himself an efficient solider in the national army, and each county is expected to see to the training and arming of its own men.'[16] Reorganisation was often left to the initiative of local commanders and organisers rather than central command. Brugha and the temporary Executive were a reference point; Volunteer units could draw encouragement from the fact that a central headquarters had been re-established, but the Executive were not in a position to offer any material support. For example, the funeral of Thomas Ashe was an important event in the reorganisation of the Dublin Brigade, as they marched with the cortege and formed a guard of honour. It was this experience, rather than any directive issued from Volunteer headquarters, that marked the re-emergence of the Dublin Volunteers.[17]

In the period between the end of the Rising and Brugha's election to Dáil Éireann in January 1919, there was a marked difference in his public and private personae. This should not be seen as a contradiction. He maintained an air of non-belligerence in public, all the while secretly rebuilding the machinery of the physical-force movement. Newspaper reports of Brugha's public speaking present a picture of a balanced individual who uses rational political arguments which often referred to geopolitical developments resulting from the on-going World War. He was fond of mentioning the Paris Peace Conference, Wilsonian principles and 'the freedom of small nations.'[18] He was, however, at the same time, engaged in a surreptitious campaign to reorganise the Volunteer movement, soon to become the IRA. He was concerned about obtaining weapons and was keen to move the struggle to the next stage, but only when the conditions were favourable. This duality is indicative of Brugha's belief that politics and war should be used in tandem in pursuit of independence.

Brugha and Count Plunkett, father of the executed 1916 leader Joseph Plunkett, were arrested on 10 June 1917 at Butt Bridge while on their way to speak at a protest. A fracas ensued as the men were being led away, during which a teenager struck Inspector Mills of the Dublin Metropolitan Police on the head with a hurley, knocking him to the ground. As Brugha was being escorted away, a Cumman na mBan medic named Lilly O'Brennan asked Brugha if she could go to the policeman's aid. According to a witness 'Cathal Brugha, who was limping by in the grip of a policeman, said, "yes, first aid."'[19] Brugha always displayed a concern for casualties but despite this, Mills later died from his injuries. Brugha and Plunkett were taken to Arbour Hill prison. This was the first and the last time Brugha was jailed. His incarceration was short lived, and the two men were released on 18 June, the same day the court-martialled Easter rebels returned. The press reported that Plunkett went straight to Westland Row train station to welcome the men home, among whom were two of his sons.[20] There is no mention of the elusive Brugha.

The return of these men injected new enthusiasm into the nationalist movement. Sinn Féin vigorously contested by-elections during the summer and de Valera was elected MP for East Clare in July. Brugha does not appear to have been involved in any campaigning. On 23 September, Brugha and de Valera addressed a large crowd at Smithfield in Dublin about the conditions faced by prisoners. In keeping with his other public utterances in 1917, Brugha was conciliatory. He said that they had not gathered 'to protest or demand. It was first and foremost to call attention to the fact that their men were being imprisoned for practicing the doctrine laid down by President Wilson.'[21] The crowd then proceeded to Mountjoy, where Rising veteran Thomas Ashe had recommenced his hunger strike; he later died in hospital as a result of force feeding.

CONVENTIONS: OCTOBER 1917

Sinn Féin held a convention on 25 and 26 October in the Mansion House. It was important for many reasons. De Valera succeeded its original founder Arthur Griffith as President, with Fr O'Flanagan and Griffith elected as vice presidents. Until the convention, Sinn Féin was still ostensibly a dual monarchist party, even though few of its members were actually committed to this policy. The Proclamation of Easter 1916 had called for a republic, and many within the movement were intent on realising this. Discussions took place between the rival factions before the convention, with Brugha, de Valera and Collins on the republican side, and Griffith and Seán Milroy on the other. A compromise was reached: it was decided that Sinn Féin would strive towards a republic, and once it had been achieved, they would allow the people to choose what form of government they wanted[22] – this constructive ambiguity would later cause enormous problems. William O'Brien told the BMH that this concept was conceived of at a meeting in Brugha's home, and the terms were drafted by de Valera. O'Brien recalled that he asked Brugha if Griffith was then prepared to accept a republic, to which Brugha replied 'he had to or walk the plank.'[23] Such a comment is characteristic of Brugha's obstinacy, a trait which contemporaries remarked on.[24] He was very reluctant to compromise his views in almost any situation.

At the convention, both de Valera and Brugha proposed their own versions of what was called a 'scheme of organisation' –

essentially the governing rules of the party. Brugha's document consisted of 18 clauses and five by-laws.[25] Ultimately, his version was rejected in favour of de Valera's, though the two documents were very similar. The meeting also saw a discussion on the appropriate use of action against British rule. An unnamed priest protested that this could cover anything from 'pitch and toss to manslaughter.' Brugha weighed in and stated 'that they did not intend to meet English rule by assassination.'[26] On the second day, the Executive committee of the party was elected (20 men and four women). MacNeill topped the poll with 882 votes – an indication that his abortive role in the Rising had not destroyed his credentials. Brugha came second with 688. Collins was the last to be elected with 340 votes – his meteoric rise was still in its early stages.[27] The convention consolidated the party 'into an organised political force'.[28]

Brugha's contributions to the convention are significant. He was involved in the negotiations to change the constitution of the party and orientating it towards a republic. He proposed a scheme of organisation. He spoke out against a policy of assassination and excessive use of force, and he used rational and logical arguments to show what he believed to be British duplicity in its treatment of Ireland. His esteemed status within the movement was recognised when he was the second person elected to the party's Executive committee. Brugha was clearly far more politically minded than the historiography has previously assumed. During the convention he appeared conciliatory, restrained and pacific. He hoped that the Republic would be recognised by world leaders in the aftermath of the on-going war in Europe he and was conscious to play down any suggestions of violent rebellion. However, in private, he continued plotting the violent overthrow of British rule in Ireland and, within six months, he was personally poised 'to meet English rule by assassination', despite his previous assurances at the Sinn Féin convention. This dual approach is indicative of his belief that both politics and violence could be used to achieve the separatists' goals, though it would be some time before Brugha would assent to the use of violence. For the time being, he favoured politics.

The next day, on 27 October, at Croke Park, the Irish Volunteers held their first convention since the Rising. De Valera was elected as president of the Volunteers, mirroring his appointment as president of Sinn Féin the previous day. Brugha was appointed Chairman of the Resident Executive, which consisted of the Dublin leadership and co-opted directors of operations – an important role. Some authors attribute the title of Chief of Staff of the Volunteers to Brugha, though it is possible that Chief of Staff and Chairman of the Resident Executive were used interchangeably.[29] In March 1918, the National Executive appointed GHQ Staff under the leadership of Richard Mulcahy, the Chief of Staff, who was in turn answerable to Brugha. When Brugha became Minister for Defence in the First Dáil, Volunteer GHQ then answered to Brugha in his role as Minister for Defence. The basis for this relationship was laid at the Volunteer Convention.[30] Both Sinn Féin and the Volunteers were now working towards the same goal, though they were not unified under a single command. Throughout the War of Independence, Brugha worked hard to subordinate the army to the Dáil.

The Volunteer convention was only about a quarter of the size of the Sinn Féin convention, but there was a considerable amount of overlap in those who attended. This was also evident at leadership level. Six of the 20 members of the Volunteer Executive were on the Sinn Féin Executive. Five of the Volunteer Executive went on to become ministers in the first two Dáils: de Valera, Collins, Brugha, Stack and Mulcahy. Maryann Valiulis has pointed out that 'the two conventions with their interlocking personnel thus synthesized and blended the constitutional and physical force traditions of Irish nationalism.'[31]

Between the end of the Rising and the end of 1917, Brugha recovered from his wounds and sought to reorganise the Volunteers. It was a period marked by politics rather than by war as Sinn Féin contested various by-elections. Brugha worked surreptitiously to rebuild the Volunteers, while publicly he urged restraint and encouraged the public to place their faith in Wilsonian principles. Foster has asserted that:

> Griffithites, nonetheless, stressed more easily negotiable themes such as over-taxation, and the need for representation in settlement negotiations after the war ended. More military-minded radicals (including, rather ambivalently, de Valera) talked of guns, drilling, reviving the spirit of Volunteering and fighting for the republic. 'Soldiers' and 'politicians' were already regarding each other suspiciously, and the implicit tension between moderate and extremist elements stretched to other issues besides that of separation from British rule.[32]

The historiography presents Brugha as the arch militarist. However, his public pronouncements in 1917 were marked by conciliation and references to the Paris Peace Conference which, according to Foster's typology, makes him a 'Griffithite.' Moreover, Foster's implication that there were two separate camps – 'soldiers' and 'politicians' belies the complexity of contemporary attitudes to violence, especially in the case of Brugha.

Sinn Féin was on the march, winning four successive by-elections in the aftermath of the Rising. These early victories were somewhat illusory however, and the electorate were not yet converted to separatism to the same extent that the 1918 General Election would portray. The IPP was not dead and buried, and they secured all three by-election seats prior to the December general election.[33] The people's 'moment of conversion' was the conscription crisis of 1918.

CHAPTER 3

The Irish Volunteers' Plan to Assassinate the British Cabinet

In the spring of 1918, it looked increasingly likely that Britain would begin conscripting Irishmen into its army to fight in the Great War. The Catholic Church, the labour movement, the Irish Parliament Party, Sinn Féin, the Irish Volunteers and a mass of public opinion were opposed to the measure. In the most audacious element of the national reaction to the conscription crisis, the Volunteers Executive planned to assassinate the British cabinet as they sat in the House of Commons. This episode has been neglected by historians who have tended to view it as a plan which was conceived of and carried out by Brugha without reference to other rebel leaders.

THE PLAN

The Irish Volunteers were controlled by a 20-man Executive elected in October 1917, which became IRA GHQ in March 1918. Among its members were de Valera, Brugha, Mulcahy, Collins and Seán McEntee.[1] With the implementation of conscription becoming more likely, the Executive met at the end of March 1918 to plan its response. Every member of the Executive was present except for Collins, who was in prison.[2] At this meeting it was decided that the IRA would execute the British government and hostile newspaper editors if conscription were introduced in Ireland. The assassins would be led by Brugha. It is most likely that Brugha conceived of the plan and proposed it to the Executive at this meeting.[3].

The BMH contains some valuable information on the mission. IRA Volunteer William Whelan told the BMH that he was summoned to a meeting in April at Parnell Square where he was interviewed by Brugha, Mulcahy and Dick McKee. A week later he returned for a follow up session, at which ten IRA Volunteers were present. This time they were briefed by Brugha and Mulcahy. As Whelan states: 'I forget whether it was Mulcahy or Cathal Brugha who first spoke giving orders that we were to go to England and kill the members of the British Government.'[4] Another Volunteer, John Gaynor, was interviewed by Mulcahy three times. Mulcahy outlined the mission, supplied him with money and a false passport, and, as Gaynor recalled, 'gave me to understand that the chances of any of the party of Volunteers surviving subsequent to those executions would be one in a million.'[5]

During April and May, the men travelled to London and were billeted in safe houses around the city. Brugha stayed in a house near Tavistock Place, about three miles from Westminster, apart from the rest of the men. At a meeting at Hampstead Heath, Brugha had the men draw coloured beads from a hat. Each bead corresponded to a minister, and so the assassins were each assigned their target. Brugha provided the men with photographs of the ministers and with weapons, and ordered the men to study the movements of their potential victims. John Gaynor was sent to Wales and insinuated himself into the area around Lloyd George's home, awaiting the arrival of the Prime Minister and the order to strike.[6] Joseph Good was assigned Bonor Law. Good recalled to the BMH that he 'was several times close on Bonar Law's heels as he walked from Downing St to the House of Parliament. I thought he was singularly incautious considering all he had done and proposed to do in Ireland. From day to day we expected orders to attack. It was very wearing.'[7] William Whelan's witness statement to the BMH includes this dramatic scene:

> [Brugha] took me into the House of Commons and we sat in the gallery. He then told me what he wanted me to do. He said 'when the time comes I will do all the shooting here at the Ministers: you keep the people back from me.' He added, 'if you can, shoot your way out. That is all I want you to do to keep the people away until I have finished the firing.' We were not armed that day. There was the usual routine work in between. We went again to the House of Commons. Cathal Brugha had a peter-the-painter down the leg of his trousers. I was unarmed. I asked him if he were going to start. He said 'No, I'm not going to start: I only want to get the feel of this thing here in the gallery.[8]

Brugha's friend and first biographer, Sceilg, claimed that Brugha recounted the London mission to him: Brugha 'went up day after day to the House of Commons and chose a place where he had good elbow room. The police and everybody helped him as he entered and left. They seemed to think he was a wounded soldier back from Flanders, and he told me they did everything they could to help him.'[9]

Tim Pat Coogan interviewed another of the assassination squad, Pa Murray, in the 1960s. Murray was tasked with executing Arthur Balfour. According to Coogan,

> One day he [Murray] learned that Balfour was to preside at Oxford at a university function that afternoon and to test his nerve he went to Oxford and accosted Balfour on the street under the pretext of seeking directions. Balfour courteously walked with him for about a hundred yards, during which Murray satisfied himself that he could have carried out his mission if he had to.[10]

Most likely, Brugha originally conceived of the assassination scheme, and he was centrally involved in the mission at all stages. However, it is imperative to point out that the Volunteer Executive unanimously endorsed the plan. Richard Walsh, a member of the Executive, told the BMH that the entire Executive signed the order to assassinate the cabinet should conscription be introduced, and he explained their rationale for doing so:

> The document we signed authorising the expedition was drawn up in such a form that its publication would explain the reasons for the action and that the members of the Executive were taking full responsibility for issuing such an order as a representative Irish authority. As soon as the action planned was carried out in England, the document with the Executive members' signatures was to be published in Ireland. This publication would be necessary to show the world that the men who carried out the operation were acting on the orders of the only body that then had the authority to authorize such actions on behalf of the Irish people, and that they were not just a crowd of gunmen acting on their own or taking orders from some unknown or obscure secret society.[11]

Tomás Ó Dochartaigh, author of the second Irish-language Brugha biography, concurs that this document was signed by the whole Executive. In his words: *'Ta an chaipéis sinn* [sic] *ann go fóil'*[12] – 'This document still exists.' Frustratingly, he provides no footnote or clue as to where it may be located. Given the explosive nature of such a document, it is far more likely that it was destroyed.

There is also evidence in the pages of *An tÓglach*, the newspaper of the Volunteers, which alludes to a consensus at the Executive level regarding the London mission. The editorial in September, 1918, addressed conscription, and states that:

The policy of the Irish Volunteers in such a contingency is, of course, a foregone conclusion. Never at any moment since the question first arose has there existed the slightest divergence of opinion among those in control of the Army of Ireland, nor among officers or men, as to their duty in case of an attempt by the enemy to enforce conscription in Ireland.[13]

In the next issue, the paper reiterated its commitment to resistance: 'In our last issue we stated clearly the unanimous decision of the Executive of the Irish Volunteers to resist conscription to the death with all the military force and warlike resources at our command.'[14] These public statements from *An tÓglach* did not, for obvious operational reasons, divulge that a team of IRA assassins were poised to take out the British government at that very moment. It is quite possible to argue that these statements in *An tÓglach* do not refer to the London mission, but rather to the other plans which the Volunteers had to resist conscription. However, when considered alongside the other available evidence in the BMH, it is quite credible that the Executive backed the plan. Conscription was never introduced in Ireland, and so this spectacular mission was aborted, though it was revived by Brugha at later stages in the War of Independence.

Historians have tended to portray Brugha as a strong advocate of violence while also harbouring a distrust of politics. This, however, is too simplistic. Politics and violence are not mutually exclusive, and Brugha used both avenues in pursuit of independence. His plan to target the British cabinet was not borne out of some kind of psychotic Anglophobia or a sense of despair at the possibility of conscription. Fundamentally, Brugha believed that politicians were responsible for the violence of their armies. As one IRA soldier who was recruited into a subsequent cabinet assassination squad by Brugha in 1920 recalled, '[Brugha] held that the men who issued the orders were the men who were responsible.'[15] He conceived of the assassination plot and returned to it at later stages because he was convinced that the ultimate responsibility for state violence lay with the government who sanctioned it. Brugha certainly was an advocate of physical force, but he was not an unthinking one.

Political assassination was a feature of international politics. The First World War had been sparked by the assassination of Archduke Franz Ferdinand. Italian anarchists killed Spanish Prime Minister Canovas and French President Carnot during the 1890s. In his recent mesmerising tracing of modern political ills to the ideals of the Enlightenment, Pankaj Mishra exposed the feeling of discontent with politics in Europe post-1870. Anarchists grew 'more conspiratorial and self-aggrandizing; the idea of "propaganda by the deed" . . . grew naturally from the suspicion that only acts of extreme violence could reveal to the world a desperate social situation and the moral integrity of those determined to change it.'[16] Brugha certainly would not have identified himself as an anarchist, but he would have approved of some of their methods. The only connection to them that we can discern is his weapon of choice – the 'Peter the Painter' Mauser was named after a Latvian anarchist.

Although Brugha revived the plan at later stages in the War of Independence, it was never carried out. Later republicans, aware of the power of 'propaganda by the deed' also resorted to political assassination. Lord Mountbatten, Ambassador Christopher Ewart Biggs and Airey Neave MP were killed in the 1970s in republican bomb attacks. The IRA targeted the British cabinet again at the Tory Party conference in Brighton in 1984. Prime Minister Margaret Thatcher survived but five people were killed.

This mission has received scant attention in the historiography to date, and when it is addressed, it is presented as a solo run by

Brugha against the better judgement of other rebel leaders. Mulcahy, in particular, has tried to distance Collins and himself from the episode. In his extensive archive, Mulcahy often refers to Brugha's wild schemes as being dreamed up autonomously and conducted independently of his colleagues in cabinet or his subordinates at GHQ. 'Cathal Brugha did no systematic work in connection with the carrying on of the military organisation. The things that filled him at any time with active intent in which he himself was to be engaged, which stand out in any way were the trips to London.'[17] However, as other evidence indicates, the IRA Executive, including Mulcahy, was in favour of the plan.

CHAPTER 4

1919: Politics and War

Brugha's revolutionary career fused both politics and force in the pursuit of independence. Nowhere is this more succinctly summed up than in his seamless transition from political assassin to public representative. Upon his return to Ireland from London, he immediately set about campaigning for the forthcoming general election set for December. Sinn Féin's decision to run him in West Waterford in the 1918 election was in keeping with their policy of only selecting Irish speakers to stand in Gaeltacht constituencies. Brugha had joined the Gaelic League in 1899[1], and, like many revolutionaries, it was his gateway into radical politics.[2] He was an accomplished Irish speaker and was noted within the League as a non-native speaker who attained great fluency.[3] He was a relatively unknown entity in Waterford, first campaigning there on 8 December 1918, though he comfortably secured his seat over the IPP incumbent, James John O'Shee, by a margin of three to one.

The election result marked a sea change in Irish politics: the IPP, so long the dominant force in nationalist politics, was swept aside by Sinn Féin, who took 73 seats compared to just 6 for the IPP – Unionists won 22, all of them in their traditional strong-holds in the North East and pockets of Dublin city. Because of the Great War, this was the first General Election to be held since 1910. The franchise had been dramatically widened and it now included women. These factors meant that many people were experiencing electoral politics for the first time, which played into the hands of the more radical Sinn Féin. The election also saw the first woman ever elected to the House of Commons – Countess Markievicz, MP for Dublin St Patricks. She, along with other Sinn Féin colleagues, refused to take her seat in the House, in keeping with their policy of abstentionism.

1919 proved to be a decisive year for the separatist movement as the basis of the counter state began to be laid. Brugha was instrumental in this, as he was centrally involved in the first meeting of the new government. In his role as Minister for Defence, he was also an important figure in the gradual progression of the Volunteers' policy from passive resistance to active guerrilla warfare. 1919 typified Brugha's dual approach to securing independence by marrying politics with war.

ELECTED, FIRST DÁIL MEETING AND SOLOHEADBEG

The inaugural session of Dáil Éireann took place on 21 January, 1919, in the Mansion House, with only 24 TDs in attendance and lasting not more than two hours.[4] Brugha was appointed Ceann Comhairle.[5] He spoke almost entirely in Irish, though reverted to English to deliver an austere message: 'We desire that there shall be no cheering whatever.'[6] Brugha declared that 'the time for talking is over in Ireland; the time for nonsensical talk is long past.'[7] This was not a call to arms, but rather a call to parliament: separatists had taken the initiative. He continued:

> Representatives from every nation have gathered in Versailles and by their own admission they have come together to bring peace to people all over the world so that no race will have to resort to war ever again. Let us boldly inform them that if they are serious in their intention

then they have no choice but to break the ties between this country and England. Unless this happens there will be no peace in Ireland.[8]

Like many of his colleagues, Brugha hoped that the Versailles talks would bring salvation for Ireland. However, he was also prepared to resist British rule in Ireland by violent means if necessary. Four important documents were read out in Irish, English and French: The Dáil Constitution; The Declaration of Independence; the Democratic Programme; and the Message to the Free Nations of the World.[9] The next day Brugha was elected 'President of the Ministry *pro tem*' and he appointed a temporary cabinet.

These meetings were well-choreographed. The use of Irish stamped an aura of distinctiveness on the proceedings, though the assembly consciously resembled other established parliamentary democracies in form. The French and English translations and the references to Versailles are indicative of the meetings' internationalist outlook. Brugha's central involvement in these historic proceedings simply cannot be reconciled with the portrait presented in the historiography of a one-dimensional gunman. Only 24 TDs attended the inaugural session, and crucially, Brugha was among them. By contrast, Collins 'found other things to do'[10]: he was in England with Harry Boland planning de Valera's jailbreak. Brugha, however, chaired the meetings, spoke with an eye on geopolitical developments, appointed a cabinet, and generally acted like a politician of a revolutionary movement.

At this juncture, Sinn Féin is best viewed as a spectrum of separatist opinion. Occupying the moderate wing were figures such as Arthur Griffith and Darrell Figgis, with Brugha on the hard-line, fundamentalist republican wing. Brugha was committed to the idea of an Irish Republic, and was, at this stage, like many of his fellow travellers, opposed to any compromise on this core political tenet. At negotiations held in his home before the Sinn

Féin Convention of October 1917, both he and de Valera had successfully argued that Sinn Féin should adopt a republican constitution. In this sense, all the Dáil meeting did was reaffirm Sinn Féin's policy. However, it is quite possible that if more moderate politicians had been in attendance on 21 January, less ambitious goals would have been set. Griffith, the political theorist of the revolution, was in prison at the time.[11] Would he have agreed to the unambiguous, and ultimately unattainable, assertion of republican status? De Valera, also incarcerated, later lamented that this first Dáil meeting had locked Sinn Féin into 'the strait jacket of the Republic.'[12] In Arthur Mitchell's view, 'if the jailed leaders had been on the scene, a different pattern of events would undoubtedly have ensued.'[14] Brugha, while certainly being politically minded, was not given to compromise or consensus. He could be blinkered, even downright obstinate, when he latched onto an idea; in 1919, his commitment to the Republic was absolute. On Brugha, Darrell Figgis commented: 'His life in the dream of the Republic – a Republic of name, without definition or constitution – was his reality. The public declaration of the name was all that to him was required to complete the reality that existed in his mind.'[13] However, one of Sinn Féin's greatest strengths in this period was its lack of political nuance. This allowed it to be the broad church to which so many voters of different political stripes could flock. Perhaps Brugha's steadfast republicanism was an asset to the burgeoning party and state in 1919.

On the same day as the first meeting of the Dáil, a group of Irish Volunteers led by Dan Breen and Séan Tracey attacked a Royal Irish Constabulary (RIC) convoy in County Tipperary, killing two policemen and making off with a quantity of gelignite. This act is generally viewed as the beginning of the War of Independence. These Volunteers had acted without prior sanction from the political wing or from the Volunteer leadership. Bringing the Volunteers, who were now more often referred to as the IRA, under the authority of both the Dáil and GHQ remained a key focus for Brugha throughout the War of Independence.

DE VALERA ESCAPES

On 3 February, Michael Collins and Harry Boland engineered the audacious escape of Éamon de Valera, Seán Milroy and Seán MacGarry from Lincoln jail using a copied key. De Valera's prison stay had been relatively comfortable as 'he spent much of his time reading and writing in his cell; his appreciation of Machiavelli's *The Prince* dates from this time. Although he exercised regularly, his aloofness and the awe he inspired among his fellow prisoners was eloquently symbolised by his playing handball alone.'[15] Following his escape, de Valera hid out in England for a few weeks, and wanted to proceed straight to America. His reluctance to return to Ireland greatly dismayed the cabinet and so Brugha was dispatched across the water where he successfully persuaded de Valera to return. Collins wanted to stage a welcoming ceremony for him, where he was to be presented with the keys to the city at Mount Street Bridge, 'his springboard to fame.'[16] Brugha and others argued against the plan as they were fearful that it might result in civilian casualties if the British intervened. Collins saw it as a lost opportunity, and wrote to Austin Stack that it was 'our Clontarf', a reference to Daniel O'Connell's perceived climb down in the face of potential British violence in 1843.[17] The time for open warfare would come later, but for now Brugha was content to await its arrival while he focused on arming, strengthening and organising the IRA.

SECOND DÁIL MEETING AND THE ARMY/DÁIL RELATIONSHIP

The second meeting of the Dáil took place between 1–4 April. Fifty two deputies attended, making it the largest sitting in the entire revolutionary period.[18] With the return of de Valera, Brugha stepped aside and de Valera became *Príomh Aire*, or President. De Valera was eminently more presidential than Brugha: he possessed a far greater political acumen and he was capable of compromise. While Brugha believed in politics as an effective means of achieving independence, his obstinacy could obstruct political progress. He was often incapable of compromise, and stated his position with finality and bluntness,[19] while de Valera was a master of circumlocution and political nuance.

The President's first act was a cabinet reshuffle, and Brugha became Minister for Defence, a post he held until the Treaty split.[20] Brugha's steadfastness was much more suited to the Department of Defence than the presidency of the Republic. It has been noted that Brugha was a relatively old revolutionary.[21] However, at the leadership level, his age was unremarkable. The average age of the cabinet was 44.5; Brugha was almost 45. Throughout the War of Independence, Brugha continued to run his candle-making business and chose to remit his ministerial salary of £350 to the Assistant Minister for Defence, Richard Mulcahy. Critics have seen this decision as a sign that Brugha was not fully committed to his government job.[22] A more sympathetic view, as expressed by James Quinn, is that Brugha preferred not to be paid[23] for what he presumably regarded as his civic duty.

At the next meeting of the Dáil, de Valera told the house that the Irish Volunteers 'had now the National Government behind them and no moral sanction further was needed. The Volunteers had placed themselves at the disposal of the elected Government of the Irish people. They would stand by that Government and would do exactly as that Government commanded them.'[24] The relationship between the army and the government, however, was not as straightforward as de Valera claimed. In a conventional government/army dyad, the Minister for Defence is in control of the armed forces and the President is in charge of the government. However, Ireland in 1919 was not conventional and, like much else, precedents and norms had yet to be established. Brugha, as Minister for Defence, spent much of the War of Independence striving to subordinate the IRA to the Dáil.

Brugha believed in the primacy of the Dáil as the elected assembly of the Irish people and, as such, the army should swear an oath of allegiance to it. However, in the words of Charles Townshend, 'beyond doubt, Brugha had reasons beyond impeccable liberal-democratic principle for pressing the oath.'[25] It is likely that he wished to assert his control over the IRA to counteract Collins' growing influence within the army. In a political sense, both men were equals as both held cabinet portfolios. However, in a military sense, Brugha, as Minister for Defence, was Collins superior, with Collins holding the subordinate position of Director of Intelligence on the GHQ staff. To complicate matters, Collins was the head of the IRB, that small, shadowy oath-bound organisation, but one that had many influential rebel leaders among its ranks. Collins also found time to run 'The Squad', a hand-picked team of assassins that operated outside of GHQ authority. Brugha's belief in the supremacy of the Dáil, coupled with his suspicions of the IRB and Collins' growing stature in the army, motivated him to secure the army's allegiance to the Dáil.

Some fraught meetings of the Volunteer Executive took place over the summer of 1919 as they argued over whether the army should take an oath of allegiance to Dáil Éireann. When the Executive finally agreed that they would take an oath, several versions were proposed but agreement could not be reached.

Brugha broke the deadlock by proposing an oath modelled on that taken by members of the American Congress and army.[26] This satisfied all concerned and IRA Volunteers (as well as government employees) swore to 'support and defend the Irish Republic, and the Government of the Irish Republic, which is Dáil Éireann, against all enemies, foreign and domestic.'[27] On 20 August, Brugha announced this development in the Dáil.[28] However, the fledging government did not find it so easy to impose its will over the dispersed army and the oath was not formally taken by many Volunteers until the autumn of 1920.[29]

Speaking in the Dáil in April, de Valera proposed a boycott of the RIC. Elaborating on this, Diarmuid O'Hegarty advised 'that they should be debarred from participation in games, sports, dances and all social functions conducted by the people.'[30] The IRA, however, was less definite in its instructions to volunteers. They were in the midst of an arms drought, something which persisted through the whole War of Independence. GHQ encouraged units to procure arms, though at this point forbade them from raiding private homes for them.[31]

Brugha and GHQ met after the Soloheadbeg shootings to discuss IRA policy. GHQ was comprised of the military chiefs who ran the army. Some of those included on the staff were Michael Collins, Director of Intelligence, and Rory O'Connor, Director of Engineering. Their direct superior was the Chief of Staff, Richard Mulcahy. Mulcahy reported to the Minister for Defence, Cathal Brugha. Mulcahy was also Deputy Minister for Defence. Brugha's role as Minister for Defence straddled both the political and military spheres of the separatist movement, though he mainly operated in the political arena. He allowed GHQ to run the war, while he represented the army at a political level. The exceptions to this were Brugha's involvements in the British cabinet assassination schemes. As Mulcahy states, 'I kept him [Brugha] advised as far as possible how far things were going without having very much more than, say, weekly contact with him at times.'[32] In general, Brugha did not engage in the minutiae of military planning, though he was consulted and involved in bigger operations and overall strategy.

Early in 1919, instructions were issued to Volunteers through their official newspaper, *An tÓglach*, edited by Piaris Béaslaí, which outlined the IRA strategy. On 31 January, the paper stated that should Volunteers be 'called on to shed their blood in defence of the new-born Republic, they will not shirk from the sacrifice.'[33] The next issue editorialised that 'Every Volunteer is entitled, morally and legally, when in the execution of his military duties, to use all legitimate methods of warfare against the soldiers and policemen of the English usurper, and to slay them if it is necessary to do so in order to overcome their resistance.'[34] These words came from Béaslaí's pen, but they 'embodied the ideas expressed by Cathal Brugha, then acting President of Dáil Éireann. They were submitted to GHQ before publication, and unanimously approved.'[35] This amounted to a policy of defensive action and active resistance, not an order for offensive warfare. Mulcahy, the IRA Chief of Staff, shared the view of the army as a defensive body in 1919, stating that 'none of us at that time ever had the idea of an open military offensive against the British, nor was it until the suppression of the Dáil in Sept 1919 that it was to any extent embarked on.'[36] Tomás Ó Dochartaigh correctly argues that Brugha was opposed to any offensive action as it would hamper Ireland's case at the Paris Peace Conference.[37]

While Brugha had an active role in the framing of the IRA's defensive policy, his department had limited control over the IRA. Historians have made it clear that local IRA leaders, acting on their own initiative, were more important drivers of military developments during the War of Independence than central planners at GHQ or Brugha as minister – this was most true in the earlier stages of the war.[38] Notwithstanding the weakness of Brugha's ministerial authority over the IRA in this period, it is clear that he saw the Volunteers as a defensive force in 1919 rather than an offensive one. This challenges the traditional portrait of him in the historiography as a strong supporter of violent action.

The arrival of de Valera in New York in June 1919 illustrated that the President now had more faith in finding a political solution to Ireland's search for independence in America rather than in Paris.[39] This change of political direction coincided with a tactical development in the military: as 1919 progressed, IRA raids on RIC barracks increased. Charles Townshend, in charting the development of guerrilla warfare in Ireland, notes that by the summer, some small, remote RIC posts had already been abandoned. By autumn, many more would follow.[40] The abandonment of these RIC stations allowed a vacuum to develop in many troubled areas, one which the IRA readily filled. One of the most important political developments in the building of the counter state in 1919 was the spread of the republican courts. This would not have been possible without the IRA action that forced the RIC withdrawal. The spread of these courts, along with the demise of the British judicial system, buttressed the legitimacy of the state in its infancy. However, the state of unrest in Ireland should not be exaggerated. According to Michael Hopkinson, 'the extremely limited and episodic nature of the hostilities during . . . 1919 scarcely merits the term "war."'[41]

REPRESSION

The British cabinet was preoccupied with the Paris Peace Conference for the first half of 1919, but, by the summer, the talks were in their final stages. In Dublin Castle, the inertia of policy makers meant there was no concerted British response to the growth of the counter state. By allowing it breathing space in its crucial early stages, Dáil Éireann had been able to establish itself as a presence in Ireland: the republican courts were a particularly potent example of this. In September, the British changed tack – they proscribed the Dáil, and followed up by banning the Volunteers, Sinn Féin, Cumman na mBan and the Gaelic League. Nationalist Ireland was now under attack and the assembly was driven underground.

In late October, Brugha wrote in Irish to de Valera in America: 'I hope you remember the scheme that I was talking about . . . when Michael and Richard were in your house. It was in my mind to put it into action again; but according to our friends it would interfere with your affairs in America. What do you think? Write to me soon.'[42] With Brugha's hopes of a hearing at the Paris talks dashed, he returned to his assassination scheme. He sent IRA scouts to London to ascertain the possibility of shooting the cabinet and newspaper editors in a co-ordinated strike. One of them reported back to Mulcahy, Collins and Brugha that he thought the mission was an 'impossibility.' Collins agreed, though Brugha 'insisted that it could and should be done', despite the fact that it would most likely result in certain death for the 30-man hit squad required for the mission.[43]

Dáil sittings became much less frequent, and the military side of the campaign was stepped up. In July, the Cork IRA leader Liam Lynch had sought GHQ's permission to attack British soldiers. This was initially refused, but was later granted, albeit with conditions attached. On 7 September, he led an attack on British forces at Fermoy, killing one soldier, wounding three, and making off with 15 rifles.[44] Though IRA attacks became more frequent in Cork, large parts of the country remained inactive. Brugha went on the run and was to remain a wanted man for the remainder of the war; he was one of the few leaders to remain at large for its duration. By October, both he and Austin Stack were living and working from 8 Landsdown Terrace, situated in a salubrious enclave of Dublin city.[45] By December 1919, he was being sought by the British under the Defence of the Realm Act.[46]

The Dublin IRA decided that the first anniversary of Armistice Day, 11 November, 1919, would be an opportune time to strike at the British forces in the capital. The army was due to parade at College Green, where Lord French was to take the military salute. IRA leader Dick McKee told Volunteer Michael McDonnell that he wanted him to execute Lord French by firing from the Bank of Ireland across the Green during the ceremony.[47] On Brugha's orders, the mission was aborted; one Volunteer who was involved claimed that they had only fifteen minutes notice.[48] It is not clear if Brugha was only notified of the attack at the last minute, or whether he changed his mind late on. Brugha was always extremely cautious about IRA action that may cause harm to civilians. At one stage, he banned the Dublin IRA from carrying out ambushes on Saturdays as there were too many shoppers on the streets.[49]

1919 had brought momentous change to Ireland. Sinn Féin had successfully rejected the Westminster parliament and established a separatist assembly. An independent Irish Republic was declared in keeping with the aspirations of the Easter rebels of 1916. Crucially, Britain's slow response allowed the separatist government to build some civic apparatus around the country. Militarily, the IRA was beginning to assert itself as a force to be reckoned with in certain parts of the country. Over the course of the year, both politicians and militarists were increasingly able to shape the direction of events in Ireland. Cathal Brugha was at the centre of this process, and he straddled both spheres of the separatist movement. As Minister for Defence, he favoured a cautious, largely defensive policy, but as British coercion was stepped up, he became increasingly willing to sanction offensive action. However,

IRA units often acted without reference to this proposed strategy. While Dáil Éireann and the IRA were trying to impose their authority on Irish affairs, Brugha was trying to impose *his* authority over the army. Personal tensions were bubbling beneath the surface, and 1920 would bring them into the open.

CHAPTER 5

1920: 'The Man with the Quare Name'

Brugha moved in the shadows in 1920. Little documentary evidence pertaining to him survives, though it is unlikely that much ever existed. He was always extremely cautious about committing anything incriminating to paper.[1] As a Minister, he only addressed the Dáil on military matters seven times, and only twice was information included on the Dáil record.[2] He attended cabinet meetings, though his reports were almost always oral; written evidence is fragmentary.[3] He moved about various safe houses, sometimes disguised as a Protestant clergyman,[4] and was always armed. Unlike many rebel leaders, he evaded capture throughout the war. The Assistant Under Secretary Alfred Cope was unsure as to who exactly Brugha was, referring to him in July 1921 as 'the man with the quare name.'[5] The British security dossier on Brugha is remarkably sparse, and their information on him prior to the truce is almost non-existent.[6] Notwithstanding this confusion, there was a warrant for his arrest and he had the handsome price of £5,000 on his head.[7]

He was constantly on the run. In the early hours of a Sunday morning in October 1920, Brugha's home at Fitzwilliam Terrace was raided. The army brought a bloodhound with them in an effort to sniff out their quarry, but only succeeded in terrifying the maid while Mrs Brugha sat in an armoured car outside. 150 soldiers careered around the street with the dog, kicking in doors and terrorising Brugha's mainly unionist neighbours.[8]

Brugha ran his ministry from Lalor's Ltd, the candle-making enterprise which he co-founded in 1909 and operated from 14 Lower Ormond Quay. He had previously worked for the church suppliers, Hayes and Finch, as a travelling salesman, but resigned because of his misgivings about working for an English-owned company. According to Tomás Ó Dochartaigh, Brugha employed some IRA men at Lalor's who knew nothing about the trade. Brugha's second floor office had a mirror pointed at the stairs so he could see who was ascending. He had a narrow ladder which led to the roof, so he could escape in case of a raid. When it was sunny, he took his work to the roof.

Some contemporaries – and indeed historians – have cast Brugha as a part-time minister because he kept working at his candle-making firm throughout the War of Independence. Arthur Mitchell has suggested that both Brugha and J. J. O'Kelly (Minister for National Language since November 1919) forwent payment as it was in keeping with the principles of the Gaelic League, of which they were both prominent members.[9] Some recalled that he was often hard to find when he was needed[10], though others report that he was readily available at his office above Lalor's.[11] However, his commitment to the separatist movement is unquestionable: he was a committed republican and never shirked physical danger during the revolution, despite the fact that he had a young family. It should be noted that Arthur Griffith, the prolific journalist, who could produce newsprint with 'manic industry'[12], also continued to work right through revolution, but the same questions regarding his diligence have not been raised.

During 1920, the IRA stepped up their campaign as the leadership approved attacks on police and barracks in January.[13] Meanwhile, Brugha and Collins sought to extend the campaign beyond Ireland's borders and wanted to establish 'foreign service flying columns.'[14] In November, they sent IRA man Seán McLaughlin to Britain where he infiltrated left-wing movements, sourced arms, conspired with Indian nationalists and generally sowed discontent. Rory O'Connor travelled to Britain to coordinate operations there, and in November the IRA announced the beginning of the campaign on British soil by burning the Liverpool docks.[15]

DÁIL AUTHORITY AND OATH

In September 1919, the Dáil agreed that the IRA should swear an oath of allegiance to the legislature. According to Florence O'Donoghue, the oath was 'administered to Volunteers at public parades of companies or smaller units during the Autumn of 1920.'[16] This was a qualified success for Brugha – he had finally brought the IRA under the nominal authority of the Dáil. In reality though, the IRA remained an army which was driven by local commanders and was not closely controlled by GHQ, let alone Dáil Éireann.[17] Later in the year, Brugha sought to reorganise the army, revamp the command structure and introduce payment for officers.[18] These measures were undertaken to enforce better discipline among the troops, but also to assert his, and the Dáil's, authority over the IRA.

In March, Brugha again returned to his cabinet assassination scheme. Three Cork-based IRA Volunteers were summoned to Vaughan's Hotel, a hub of revolutionary planning, where they met with Collins and Brugha. Collins joked with the men and bought them a drink. 'Brugha', recalled one of them, 'spoke in an austere manner and emphasised the dangers and trials with which we might have to contend.'[19] Brugha oversaw the military planning and Collins took care of the finances. This may be a reason why some have questioned his commitment to his ministerial duties. One Cork commander recalled that he only received one communication from Brugha throughout the whole war. The exception to this seems to be the cabinet assassination plan. In 1918, 1920 and 1921, Brugha personally planned and organised assassination attempts. On this occasion, the plan was postponed when it seemed likely that the British were offering the prospect of negotiations.

In May 1919, Harry Boland arrived in America as an envoy of both Dáil Éireann and the IRB. Upon de Valera's arrival the following month, Boland acted as the travelling president's 'private secretary, tour organiser, bagman, political adviser, butler, and personal entertainer.'[20] The multifarious Boland was also an enthusiastic, though inept, arms smuggler. The gun-running operation was ostensibly under the authority of the Minister for Defence, though in reality it was conducted through the IRB and their American contacts.[21] On 11 August, Boland wrote to Brugha from the American capital to inform the Minister that he had received quotations for weapons and could secure transport 'if ye [*sic*] are prepared to accept delivery' while also assuring him that 'we have not forgotten your views in certain contingences for a world action.'[22] Boland's biographer, David Fitzpatrick, a historian who is well acquainted with Boland's quirky coded letters and enigmatic messages, has suggested that Brugha was awaiting a decision from de Valera regarding the British cabinet assassination scheme.[23] It is not clear if de Valera sanctioned the plan before it was eventually shelved.

BLOODY SUNDAY

Bloody Sunday, 21 November 1920, was one of the deadliest days of the war, with a catalogue of killings punctuating the day. At 9 am, members of the Dublin Brigade of the IRA, accompanied by IRA intelligence officers and the men of Michael Collins' squad, entered the private residences and boarding houses where several alleged members of the British intelligence network were staying.

Fourteen men (including two auxiliary policemen who interrupted the raid on Mount Street) were shot dead. A fifteenth man died later of the wounds he sustained that morning.[24] That afternoon, police, army and auxiliaries raided Croke Park during a football match, where they killed at least 12 civilians. In the evening, two senior Dublin IRA commanders, Peadar Clancy and Dick McKee, and a civilian, Conor Clune, were shot in Dublin Castle, where they had been imprisoned since the previous night.

Bloody Sunday reveals interesting insights into Brugha's attitudes to violence. He seems to have agreed with the mission in principle, though he did remove some names from the hit list on the grounds that he believed that there was not sufficient evidence against them.[25] According to Ernie O'Malley, Brugha 'was very conscientious and adamant in his judgement. If to his mind there was the slightest loophole for uncertainty about an agent or spy, then the individual could not be dealt with.'[26] Notwithstanding his vetting of the victims, at least one was innocent, having only come to Dublin to trade horses.[27] While Brugha could often display deep concern that individuals were targeted when they should not have been, he could equally exhibit an almost total disregard for his own life.

Following the morning's operations, Mulcahy and Brugha were holed up in a safe house together near Mountjoy Square. Mulcahy recalled Brugha's reaction to hearing soldiers outside:

> What does Cathal do but went [sic] up to his room, pulled up the window, pulled over a chair alongside it, pulled out two revolvers and put them on the bed beside him, and took off his boots! . . . Now, my tactics would have been entirely different. I would have [had] my bicycle out and been out of the gate at the back, and I would have been off up Drumcondra; but, noblesse oblige, I had to sit alongside my minister on the side of the bed there, praying whatever was going to pass.[28]

Brugha then moved his hiding place up the road, to the grounds of Temple Street Hospital, where a caretaker happened upon him, sitting at a table in an outhouse, again with his two revolvers. He informed Brugha that the area was surrounded by soldiers, to which Brugha responded, 'If those people come in, you will find my dead body . . . and don't be surprised to find six or seven of the bodies of our visitors.'[29]

The erroneous assertion that Brugha had little time for politics is often presented alongside his apparent strong commitment to physical force, as if the former proves the latter.[30] However, he had complex and well-thought-out attitudes to violence, and was not simplistically bloodthirsty. He expressed regret that war was necessary to secure British withdrawal[31], and it is clear that he had reflected on the legitimacy of violence and where that violence should be directed. He detested civilian casualties and had been slow to sanction IRA attacks on non-military targets, including police and intelligence personnel. He would not allow the execution of women spies.[32] The IRB's raison d'être was to wage war to secure an Irish republic, though Brugha was opposed to it because it was an unelected secret society. He believed that politicians were ultimately responsible for the actions of the army. He returned to his cabinet assassination scheme throughout the war because it was the cabinet who were the ultimate arbiters of political violence in Ireland. It was this idea of political responsibility which, in part, informed his efforts to cement IRA allegiance to the Dáil. Brugha believed in the primacy of the Dáil and the importance of politics. By combining politics with insurrection, he believed that Ireland could win its independence.

Notwithstanding these qualifications of Brugha's bellicosity, if the circumstance warranted it, he had no issue with taking up arms himself. At times, his actions bordered on the suicidal. During the Rising, his body riddled with shrapnel and bullets, he propped himself against a wall, shouting, 'Come on, you cowards, till I get one shot before I die. I am only a wounded man'.[33] If he had opened fire in the House of Commons viewing gallery in 1918, he certainly would have been killed, as he admitted himself, though he also defiantly believed that he 'would do one of them anyway.'[34] The Bloody Sunday vignettes reveal a detached, calm Brugha, contemplatively waiting for soldiers to burst through the door and shoot him up. He never considered surrender; if his enemies wanted to capture him, they would have to kill him first. This was reminiscent of Ceannt's last letter to republicans to 'never treat with the enemy'.[35] His absolute refusal to countenance surrender was another aspect of his deep-seated obstinacy. Intransigence was his *hamartia*: it obstructed his politics, damaged his working relationships with both military and political leaders and ultimately led to his bloody demise during the Civil War.

THE BRUGHA–COLLINS CONFLICT

During de Valera's American sojourn, Griffith acted as President until he was arrested in the wake of Bloody Sunday. Griffith nominated Brugha as his successor, though Brugha demurred because of workload pressures in the Department of Defence, and so the role went to Collins, who only held the post for two weeks until de Valera returned to Ireland on 23 December.[36] During his 18-month absence, much had changed. The war had intensified, the Dáil had been driven underground and tensions were brewing between key rebel leaders. On the night of his return, de Valera met Brugha at a house on Dublin's Merrion Square. De Valera chided Brugha for carrying a *Mauser* pistol on him, telling his minister that if he 'were held up for examination in the street the gun would be found on him or he would be compelled to use it under very disadvantageous circumstances.' Brugha would not be persuaded, and replied that he 'intended to use the gun if there was any question of his being held up.'[37]

It was at this meeting that de Valera first became aware of the growing rift between Brugha and Collins. Their differences arose, according to de Valera, from Brugha seeking to bring the IRA under the authority of the Dáil and Brugha's distrust of the IRB, wherein Collins was president of its Supreme Council. Brugha was glad of de Valera's return, for he feared 'otherwise there would be a split from top to bottom.'[38] The President, however, 'did not regard the difference between Brugha and Collins as being of a dangerous character, and proceeded to ignore them.'[39]

Tension had been simmering between the two men since at least August 1919 when Brugha successfully secured Dáil approval for an IRA oath. Brugha had left the IRB after 1916, wishing instead that the IRA become an open military movement.[40] Collins and Mulcahy believed that a strategy of guerrilla warfare and assassination were more effective. They were correct in this summation: it was inconceivable that the IRA could have combated the British army as effectively as they did if they had done so conventionally.

Like many politicians, both Brugha and Collins possessed strong personalities; these personalities did not complement each other. Collins was a young man from a rural background and was gregarious and boisterous. Brugha was a middle-class Dublin man, 16 years older and struck his contemporaries as austere, stoic and laconic.[41] Brugha was an abstainer, having quit drinking in 1917 because of his displeasure at contributing to Her Majesty's Treasury through taxation on alcohol.[42] Neither did he smoke or swear. Collins was a veritable expert at all three. Brugha was a devout Catholic, while Collins 'was actively anti-clerical for much of his life, and blamed the Catholic Church for many of Ireland's problems.'[43] Some people recalled Brugha as polite and gentle, while others remarked on his cold and aloof manner.[44] Collins seemed to possess an uncanny ability to make friends and inspire loyalty. Brugha's steely stubbornness meant that once he had made his mind up on Collins, it was highly unlikely that he would change it. According to Béaslaí, 'on every issue he [Brugha] made up his mind on a small number of data, and crystallised them into a formula, and all subsequent attempts to put before him fresh data or considerations he had ignored were only a waste of time.'[45]

The two men also clashed over power. As Minister for Defence, Brugha was constantly striving to assert his ministerial control over the IRA, while Collins used his IRB connection to exert his authority of the military. 'These confused relationships between institutions encouraged the emergence of contending and charismatic leaders. Sinn Féin, the Volunteers and the IRB provided powerbases for ambitious men.'[46]

Mulcahy, who was an ally of Collins and would himself later fall foul of Brugha, believed that the fractious power struggle had come about because of the confusing nature of the IRB relationship to both the Dáil and the IRA. Collins 'had surrounded himself, in the IRB tradition, with groups of men who accepted his leadership totally and his word as law in a kind of charismatic union.'[47] But Mulcahy also attributed a more human quality to Brugha's antipathy towards Collins, claiming that de Valera had said to him: 'do you know I think that Cathal is jealous of Mick . . . Isn't it a terrible thing that a man with the qualities that Cathal undoubtedly has, so should fall a victim to a dirty little vice like jealously.'[48] Mulcahy agreed with this assessment. De Valera's own archive does not record that this was his point of view. Patrick Murray has shown that de Valera policed his archive to present a certain image of himself to historians, but also that de Valera and Mulcahy could have radically different interpretations of the revolution.[49] This allusion to jealousy has crept into the historiography. It is undeniable that Brugha harboured a growing animosity towards Collins, which eventually exploded into a personal attack during the fractious Treaty debates. However, the antipathy was borne of a personality clash and was amplified by a power struggle.

1920 was a violent year: the forces of the crown lost 525 men and almost 1,000 were wounded.[50] The authorities recognised the effectiveness of the IRA and there were whisperings of settlement talks towards the end of the year.[51] Brugha had moved closer to asserting his and the government's authority over the army when the oath was administered in the autumn. But the year was not a total success for Brugha: his relationship with Collins deteriorated and, before long, he would also fall out with Mulcahy.

CHAPTER 6

1921

In 1921 Brugha once again returned to his pet project: the assassination of the British cabinet. This time, he picked the Longford IRA commander Seán MacKeon, 'who had already earned a name for intrepid fighting marked by an almost reckless humanity for the enemy wounded'[1] to lead the mission, and summoned him to Dublin for a meeting. MacKeon travelled to Dublin and met Brugha at Lalors. He recalled that he was greeted in a businesslike manner and then rigorously questioned about military matters in his area: 'his questions impressed me as a man who was nothing if not capable and thorough.'[2]

MacKeon was put in charge of a squad which he would lead to London in order to kill the cabinet. The particulars were left to him, though Brugha stipulated that each assassin was to be assigned a minister, just as had been the case in 1918. Brugha's explanation of his motivation for the plan again reveals insights into his attitudes to violence and his belief that politicians were ultimately responsible for the military actions of the armies which they controlled.

If you wiped out every Black and Tan in Ireland to-morrow, you'd have shiploads of them pouring in again, the day after! And if you wiped every soul of them out, double as many shiploads would come in, the day after that! . . . To save Ireland, you have got to wipe out the guilty ones who sent the Black and Tans here! We have got to wipe out every member of the British Cabinet.[3]

The conditions under which MacKeon would have to operate would be far more difficult than had been the case when Brugha led the mission in 1918. The burning of the docks at Liverpool, and Bloody Sunday in Dublin, had shocked the British establishment and, as a result, they had dramatically increased their security: boats patrolled the Thames, barricades were erected in front of Downing Street and armed detectives stalked about Westminster.[4]

After meeting Brugha, MacKeon then went to see Collins, who was shocked to hear that the London plan had been revived. He rebuked MacKeon, telling him to stop 'thinking you are some vest-pocket Bonaparte going over to conquer England. Let me tell you that your mad plan was put before the Defence Council, and the Cabinet, and was scouted out.'[5] He ordered him to return to Longford and Collins would explain to the Minister for Defence that he was countermanding his orders.[6] Collins' support for such drastic action had diminished as the war intensified but the British establishment remained terrified by such a possibility. Indeed, when Field Marshal Wilson was killed in 1922, Winston Churchill was so alarmed that he took to sleeping in his attic, armed with a revolver, and barricaded himself in with iron sheets.[7]

By this stage, relations between Collins and Brugha were poisonous. They had clashed on military matters before, but now Collins was directly interfering in Brugha's portfolio. MacKeon departed for Longford, though was shot and captured on the journey. He was sentenced to death, and Collins repeatedly engineered escape attempts.[8] MacKeon earned the sobriquet 'the Blacksmith of Ballinalee' and his release became a sticking point in Anglo-Irish negotiations when truce terms were being arranged.

RELATIONSHIPS: BOLAND, COLLINS AND MULCAHY

De Valera's return to Ireland from the USA in 1920 had reinvigorated the underground government: he introduced holidays for employees, tried to ban smoking in government offices and established a more secure and effective filing system.[9] As a result, far more correspondence from Brugha from this period is available. In America, Harry Boland continued his arms smuggling attempts during 1921. On 2 March, Brugha wrote to Boland, requesting more weapons and ammunition: 'I will send you authority for the spending of any amount you name . . . If we can get enough goods to keep us going I believe without any apprehension that we are going to knock [blacked out] out of them.'[10]

Boland expected to ship 150 Thompson machine guns in the following weeks, which he had already purchased, but they were seized by US authorities. This incident typified the calamitous nature of Boland's ill-fated arms smuggling enterprise. Another 495 guns were ready to be shipped from Hoboken, New Jersey, though these were impounded by the harbour master there.[11] Boland also raised a foreign legion to fight in Ireland, something which was 'central to [his] conspiratorial strategy'[12], telling Brugha that 'we have up to one hundred men here, young Irish Americans, most of them born in Ireland, who have seen service overseas, many of them with distinction, and everyone one of them are the right type.'[13] Two were sent to Ireland to instruct the IRA in the use of the Thompsons. Brugha told Boland that the IRA would 'size them up' before any more decorated American Great War veterans were dispatched.[14] A later letter reveals that the IRA were suitably impressed and would welcome more, though the truce meant they never travelled.[15] Brugha's letters to Boland are courteous but impatient. He was desperate for more munitions and was less concerned with excuses or optimistic estimates.

Brugha's concerns over accounting issues begin to emerge within his correspondence with Boland. In March, Brugha asked for 'invoices with all stuff in future if possible and let me know how much money you have spent.'[16] Later, Brugha enquired of Boland why 'a considerable sum – between 200,000 and 300,000 dollars – has been drawn out of my vote. Kindly say if this is correct, and if correct, please explain.'[17] Brugha's tone is gentle and friendly, and he seems to trust in Boland's integrity and his handling of the finances, despite his IRB connections. Perhaps Boland's likable character goes some way in explaining Brugha's relatively relaxed approach. He reassured his American gun runner: 'I don't rail at people, and if I ever do, you will not be the man I'll start on.'[18] The accounting concerns are significant as 1921 also saw discrepancies in Collins' accounts for guns in Scotland, though Brugha's actions in that matter were far removed from the understanding manner with which he addressed Boland.

For the first 18 months of the War of Independence, the Department for Defence did not appropriate any funds for military activities – IRA units were expected to finance themselves. 'From June 1920 the Dáil began appropriating gradually increasing sums for the military. In the decisive six-month period preceding the truce of July 1921 the Departent of Defence estimated expenses at £32,750 and spent £39,350. By any standard, this was revolution on the cheap.'[19] It was this increase in interaction between the departments of Defence and Finance which may go some way in explaining why Brugha and Collins came to blows now, rather than earlier.

In January, Brugha raised his concerns at a cabinet meeting that some monies which had been earmarked to buy weapons in Glasgow had gone missing. The complaint was directed at Collins in his role as Minister for Finance. In February, Collins wrote to de Valera to complain about his treatment at the hands of Brugha, saying that 'it is not gentlemanly' and that Brugha was 'raking up petty technicalities.'[20] Brugha informed the President that he regarded the missing £2,700 'a very serious situation'.[21] It was not an inconsequential sum however, as inflation during the Great War had caused enormous fluctuation in the purchasing power of the pound.[22] For the purposes of comparison with Harry Boland's accounting discrepancies, it is useful to point out that £2,700 was equal to $10,395 in 1921.[23] This incident reveals the inconsistent approach which Brugha took with Collins when compared to his understanding treatment of Boland in America. Compared to the $200,000 – $300,000 unaccounted for in America, this was petty. Brugha 'would continue his Javert-like pursuit almost until his death, dragging in de Valera, the GHQ, the cabinet and eventually, and in public, the Dáil.'[24] According to one account, de Valera presided over an investigation which vindicated Collins, but nonetheless left him in tears, with Brugha storming out, refusing to shake hands.[25] The quibbling over money, the dogged pursuit of answers and the refusal to patch things up with Collins are again indicative of Brugha's deep-seated intransigence and his refusal to compromise. The investigation into the missing money meant that arms smuggling through British channels was impeded.[26] This episode forms part of Brugha's vendetta against Collins. Trouble had been brewing between the two for years and now it manifested itself. Rather dramatically, Coogan has suggested that the feud 'was to be a causal factor in creating Civil War'.[27] This is both an exaggeration and a simplification.

As with Collins, Brugha's relationship with Mulcahy also began to deteriorate in the first half of 1921. In a lengthy correspondence regarding the relationship between the IRA, the republican police and Dáil courts in North Longford, we can see the animosity growing between them. Both men exercised restraint, with Brugha writing to Mulcahy that 'the main thing is to be patient and forbearing with one another until we have reached our goal.'[28] This tense relationship would not last the year, and Brugha sacked Mulcahy during the truce.[29] Although the guns fell silent on 11 July for the truce, the deep divisions within the rebel movement were becoming irrevocable.

HEALTH PROBLEMS AND PHILOSOPHICAL DIFFERENCES

Brugha's health never fully recovered after his near-death experience during the Rising. In 1921, he was under immense pressure, like many of his colleagues in the separatist movement. In a letter to de Valera in March,[30] he complained of a cold, and during the summer he wrote to Boland that all in Dublin were terribly overworked.[31] Collins was in a similar state: 'overstretched and often ill . . . prone to bouts of flu, and seems to have developed chronic stomach and kidney problems that could leave him bedridden or functioning in great discomfort.'[32] Perhaps matters were overwhelming Brugha in 1921, affecting his relationships with both Collins and Mulcahy. It was also the case that he had worked with them for five years at this stage and the differences which they may have been able to work around were becoming more pronounced. In 1921, months before the truce, the political divisions which became so evident as a result of the Treaty can be traced through the personal relationships among the leadership at this time. By the summer, Brugha's relationships with Collins and Mulcahy were in ruins, Austin Stack resented Collins, and de Valera had to work hard to maintain unity. Brugha's ill health can perhaps go some way towards explaining his fractious relationship with some rebel leaders.

The philosophical differences relating to military policy were also coming to a head. At an April meeting at The O'Rahilly residence, 40 Herbert Park, military and political leaders agreed to a large-scale attack on the Customs House.[33] This was the kind of action which de Valera and Brugha favoured, and it is possible that this attack was their brain-child.[34] Mulcahy has recorded his opposition to the operation, claiming that he felt he was 'dragged' along with it.[35] De Valera's return from the United States the previous Christmas strengthened Brugha's hand in matters like this. In late March, de Valera announced that the Dáil accepted responsibility for the actions of the IRA. This was another step towards Brugha's goal of achieving an orthodox relationship between the government and the army.[36] In the General Election of May, 1921, Brugha topped the poll in Waterford-Tipperary East and retained his cabinet portfolio.

Brugha was actively and energetically seeking arms from American, European and African sources in the first half of 1921.[37] When de Valera was captured in June, documents in his possession from the Department of Defence revealed that the rebels were planning on intensifying the war effort.[38] Many, including Brugha, saw the truce as a temporary cessation.[39] The first half of 1921 was bittersweet for Brugha. He had come closer to asserting ministerial control over the army, and the IRA had succeeded in forcing the British to the negotiating table. He must have counted these as successes. But the truce did not bring tranquillity; the feud with Collins and Mulcahy simmered on through the summer.

CHAPTER 7

Truce to Civil War

During the cessation, Brugha continued to source arms from abroad but Boland's American gun-running efforts continued to flounder. On 19 July, he wrote to Brugha complaining that he 'had no help or co-operation from your department; every man carrying stuff from America was originally picked up by me, although I have asked time and again for help to land the tremendous amount of goods we have here.'[1] However, Boland did have 25 former American Officers ready to send to Ireland but held off as he wanted to see how the truce developed before dispatching them. He regretted that more arms had not reached Ireland safely and closed with 'Congratulations to you as Head of the Army of the Republic on the wonderful results achieved.'[2] By this stage, of Boland's promised 653 Thompson machine guns, over 400 had been captured and only 15 had made it into IRA hands in Ireland. He was later charged by Brugha for misuse of funds.[3]

Efforts to import arms from Berlin were also scuppered, this time by spies. Notwithstanding these setbacks, the Truce proved to be a busy and productive time for the army. Brugha received a report from the Quartermaster General's (QMG) Department informing him that the arms importation in the first five months of the truce exceeded those in the eleven months prior to it. The amount of explosives they held had doubled and far more money was being spent on munitions. They were spending more money, making more homemade grenades and had doubled their holding of explosives. Brugha must have been hounding the QMG to increase their arsenals as the report closes with 'This statement should prove that there has been no slackness or neglect of duty in the department. The Truce brought with it no facility for the department which had to carry out the greater portion of its work as under war conditions.' It concluded by pointing out that 'the only advantage of the Truce was the freedom of movement and the advantage of being able to work at night as well as day.'[4]

FEUD WITH MULCAHY AND COLLINS

With the war against the British in abeyance, Brugha stepped up his campaign against Collins and Mulcahy. The occasion of the next battle was the unfair dismissal of an ex British-army officer named Robbie who operated the Yost typewriter company in Dublin. A member of the Dublin Brigade had exiled him from the country and he was now in Britain. Just as he had done before Bloody Sunday, Brugha sought proof of the man's guilt. None was forthcoming, and Collins and Mulcahy agreed with him that Robbie should be allowed to return to Ireland.

Both Mulcahy and Collins were entwined in the episode as Collins was head of Intelligence and Mulcahy as Chief of Staff was responsible for the day-to-day running of the army. Unhappy with how the matter was being handled by them, Brugha sent a scathing letter on 30 July: 'The handling of this case from start to finish – even to yesterday's letter, signed I/O GHQ displays an amateurishness that I thought we had long outgrown.'[5] Mulcahy's indignant reply came five weeks later:

> I consider that the tone of your letter of 30th July very unfortunate, and must have a very destructive influence on the harmony and

discipline of the staff, and unless something can be done to eliminate the tendency to revert to this tone when differences arise, I cannot be responsible for retaining harmony and discipline among the staff.[6]

Brugha was furious, writing to Mulcahy:

The concluding paragraph of your note is scarcely worthy of notice, and I would not refer to it at all, expect that if I passed it without comment, you might be tempted to write in the same strain a second time; and it is only fair to warn you that should such occur, I shall very seriously consider the advisability of suspending, if not terminating, your connection with this Department.

What good purpose was served by your writing thus 5 weeks after the event is probably known to yourself. To me it seems a further development of that presumption on your part that prompted you to ignore for some months past the duly appointed Deputy Chief of Staff. However, before you are very much older, my friend, I shall show you that I have as little intention of taking direction from you as to how I should reprove inefficiency or negligence on the part of yourself or the D/I, as I have of allowing you to appoint a Deputy Chief of Staff of your own choosing.

In regard to your inability to maintain harmony and discipline among the staff: it was scarcely necessary to remind me of the fact, as your shortcomings in that respect – so far at least as controlling the particular member already mentioned [Collins] is concerned – have been quiet apparent for a considerable time.[7]

This was Brugha at his worst. He is hectoring and patronising and should have had more respect for his seasoned and competent Chief of Staff. Mulcahy appealed to de Valera to intervene, though he was evidently unable to rectify the situation. A week later, Brugha wrote to Mulcahy, informing him that 'until further notice your services will not be required by this Department.'[8]

ARMY REORGANISATION

Brugha took the opportunity of the Truce to reorganise the army. On 15 September, 1921 the cabinet agreed to the reorganisation of the 'New Army'. The old Volunteer executive met and dissolved itself with the new army set to come into being on 25 November, the anniversary of the foundation of the Volunteers. Some of the participants in this process might have cast their minds back to how harmonious things seemed then, in 1913, when they were all united and working towards an ill-defined separation from Britain. On 16 November, Brugha wrote to Mulcahy, who he now addressed as 'Risteard O'Maolchatha T. D.', rather than his title C/S (Chief of Staff) as he usually did. He then offered him a different role of Chief of Staff and rank of Commander General in the newly organised army.

Mulcahy questioned some of the appointments and the process in which appointments would be made in the future. As Chief of Staff, he wanted to have the right of appointment to his own staff. This was reasonable, as he would be working with them and wanted to have people he knew he could trust and rely on. Brugha, however, wanted to assert his ministerial authority and appoint men of his choosing to GHQ staff. He had previously tried to get his ally Austin Stack onto GHQ as Deputy Chief of Staff. As he pointed out to Mulcahy in the Robbie row, Mulcahy had been ignoring that appointment and was now trying to appoint his own Deputy.

The army reorganisation caused further confusion in the provinces. Seán MacEoin wanted to communicate with Mulcahy before he accepted the offer of a commission in the new force.[9] A surprised Dan Horgan of the 5th Northern Division wanted a similar clarification from Mulcahy.[10] Frank Aiken, Commander of the 4th Northern Division, recalled that the offer of his new commission was the first contact he had ever had with the Minister for Defence. On 25 November, the day the fledgling new army was to come into being, de Valera chaired a joint meeting of GHQ and cabinet at the Mansion House in an attempt to clarify issues and resolve differences. The President eventually lost his patience and ended the meeting when he 'pushed the small table in front of him and declared in a half-scream, half-shout "ye [sic] may mutiny if ye like, but Ireland will give me another army."'[11]

The tensions between civil and military authorities at his stage are again indicative of the fluid nature of the roles of the various bodies and relationships between them. In the breathing space afforded by the Truce, various actors had attempted to solidify their standing in, and accrue as much advantage to, their respective positions. Both Brugha and Mulcahy wanted the sole right to appoint men to GHQ staff as they saw it as part of their briefs. The reticence on the part of some officers to accept the new commissions reflects the esteem in which Mulcahy was held. It had been the army who had won the government an opportunity to negotiate with the British, an army of which Mulcahy had been Chief of Staff. Mulcahy also knew the divisional commanders much better than Brugha and had built rapport and relationships with them over the course of the War of Independence. Brugha usually liked to stay out of the day-to-day running of the army, but he used the opportunity of the Truce to try to establish communications with more IRA commanders.[12] Perhaps he felt he would need to rely on their loyalty in the near future.

The formation of the New Army was ultimately a stillborn enterprise – the status quo prevailed. Mulcahy wrote to divisional commanders that 'it might be inferred . . . that a New Army is being formed, this is not really so.'[13] More pressing matters were beginning to take precedence. Talks would soon begin between British and Irish negotiators, and de Valera was pondering who to send to represent his government's case. The last time Brugha had been in London, he was armed and intent on assassinating the British cabinet. Now, he flatly refused to go to the talks. In any case, his uncompromising character would have been entirely unsuited to such a delicate diplomatic mission. Collins tried to argue that he was a simple solider and would also be unsuited to the task, but he went anyway. De Valera claimed that he had to stay in Ireland to convince the hard-line republicans like Brugha and Stack that compromise was necessary.[14]

The negotiating team, made up of Collins, Griffith, Robert Barton, Eamonn Duggan and George Gavan Duffy, were given confusing and contradictory instructions. They were plenipotentiaries which meant they were entitled to sign a Treaty, but they were also told that any potential agreement had to be sent to the cabinet in Dublin for approval. When Lloyd George threatened the prospect of 'war within three days', the five men signed the Treaty in the early hours of 6 December.[15] Collins later correctly claimed that the Treaty would have to be ratified by the Dáil before it come into effect, but the signatories were accused of reneging on their promise to submit any agreement to cabinet before signing. Some even accused them of treason – a caustic insult to the character of those who had laboured and fought for Irish freedom for so many years. On 6 December Brugha, Mulcahy and de Valera were in the west of Ireland inspecting troops when they heard the surprising news that the Treaty had been signed. The impending split was ominously illustrated on their return train journey to Dublin, with Brugha and de Valera sitting in one carriage and Mulcahy in another.

THE TREATY AND THE DÁIL

The highly-charged Treaty debates took place at Earlsfort Terrance between 14 December 1921 and 7 January 1922. The Treaty proposed an Ireland which had dominion status, with members of Parliament swearing an oath of allegiance to the Crown. Britain would retain control of three deep-water ports on the Atlantic seaboard and a Boundary Commission would to be established to decide on the future position of the border with Northern Ireland. Crucially, the new state would not be a Republic. De Valera, leader of the opposition to the Treaty, introduced his idea of External Association – embodied in Document No. 2 – as an alternative. He had claimed in the months previous that 'we are not doctrinaire republicans' and this document proved his assertions, for it fell short of an Irish Republic. He proposed that Ireland would be independent but operate in association with the British Commonwealth in some matters such as defence. Brugha spoke in favour of the proposal, showing that he too was not 'doctrinaire.' This is significant as it illustrates that Brugha was in fact capable of compromise. Máire Comerford witnessed Brugha's speech in favour Document No. 2, and recalled the great effort it took from him turn his back on the republican ideal:

> I listened attentively for he spoke under great strain. It is still clear in my memory. When we came out from the chamber in Earlsfort Terrace, I met him in the passage. It had taken great effort for him to make such a speech. I was unable to congratulate him or say anything he may have expected to hear. His lips were blue; I remember how blue they appeared as he held himself tensely.[16]

During the Treaty debates, Brugha's antipathy for Collins was out in the open. He has been much criticised[17] for his denunciation of Collins, who he claimed had sought notoriety. Brugha said that the press had falsely claimed that Collins was 'the man who won the war'[18] when in fact he was 'merely a subordinate in the Department of Defence.'[19] According to Todd Andrews, a few vacillating deputies aligned with the pro-Treaty side in the wake of the attack. Brugha's comments were motivated, not by jealously, but rather by his hostility to Collins and to the Treaty. In a statement to the House, he said that:

> A Deputy from Tipperary and Waterford, one of my own colleagues, has sent me in a question which I will read. 'In view of the fact that many members and several people are biased in favour of this proposed Treaty because the Minister of Finance is in favour of ratification, and in view of the fact that many of these people, and many of these members, are of the opinion that Mr. Michael Collins is a leader of the army and has fought many fights for the Republic, I think it is of great importance that an authoritative statement be made (a) defining the real position Mr. Michael Collins held in the army, (b) telling what fights he has taken an active part in, provided this can be done without injustice to himself or danger to the country; or can it be authoritatively stated that he ever fired a shot at any enemy of Ireland?[20]

Brugha claimed that he was concerned that Collins' lofty status would sway many in favour of the Treaty. Indeed, later some people would claim they supported the Treaty because 'if it's good enough for Mick, it's good enough for me'.[21] It is undeniable that Brugha possessed ferocious animosity towards Collins, and this goes some way in explaining the bitterness in the attack. However, Brugha was not jealous of Collins' fame. Brugha was naturally retiring and 'loathed limelight'.[22] In fact, he deliberately avoided the spotlight, preferring to remain in the shadows of the revolutionary movement. Secrecy suited his reserved demeanour and his ministerial brief.

Following the Christmas recess, the Dáil voted 64 to 57 to accept the Treaty on 7 January. Two days later, de Valera led a walkout of anti-treaty TDs, and the provisional government was formed less than a week after with Michael Collins as Chairman. Richard Mulcahy took Brugha's old role and became Minister for Defence. As people on both sides tried to find a way around the impasse, events in Belfast spiralled out of control. The partition issue had been largely ignored by TDs during the Treaty debates, but the reality of sectarian divisions was clear with over 100 people killed in February and March.[23] Few could see it at the time, occupied as they were by the symbolism of oaths and the status of the republic, but the Northern question would become the most enduring legacy of the Treaty.

A general election was scheduled for June. In an effort to heal the split caused by the Treaty, Collins and de Valera arranged a pact, whereby pro- and anti-Treaty Sinn Féin coalition candidates would be nominated based on their existing numbers in the Dáil. Long before polling day, republicans were questioning the legitimacy of the election. They argued that the vote was not a free one, as the British had threatened war if the Treaty had not been signed. Republicans also wanted the election to be held on a 32-county basis but were of course denied this. The franchise had been widened for the 1918 election and had gone some way in boosting Sinn Féin support. The anti-Treaty side were now pushing for universal adult suffrage (only women over 30 could vote at the time). In the Dáil, Brugha asserted that 'from his knowledge of women in public affairs . . . they had as true an insight in national matters as men.'[24] This was political opportunism – Brugha was no feminist – and was based on the assumption that young women were radical and would vote against the Treaty. But while Brugha could promote the cause of women's rights if it favoured his position on the Treaty, prominent suffragette Jennie Wyse Power could just as easily jettison her feminism in the context of the national question: she was in favour of the Treaty. Interestingly, she shared Brugha's assumption that young women would vote against the settlement and so would not support the calls for them to be allowed to vote. In the words of Cal McCarthy, 'one of the great political debates of the early twentieth century was, temporarily at least, breaking down along pro- and anti-Treaty lines.'[25]

THE TREATY AND THE ARMY

In the months following the Treaty split, both the IRA and the Dáil continued in existence, alongside the provisional government and the nascent Free State army. The majority of the IRA was opposed to the Treaty, and they were in a stronger position in terms of numbers of men compared to the new Free State army. The Free State army was ostensibly loyal to the provisional government, though this loyalty had not yet been tested. Through the early months of 1922, they were busy recruiting and installing themselves into the recently vacated British barracks.

In the vacuum created by the departing British, anti-Treaty IRA units also managed to seize some British barracks. They were becoming a law onto themselves. As far as they were concerned, they had sworn to 'support and defend the Irish Republic, and the Government of the Irish Republic, which is Dáil Éireann, against all enemies, foreign and domestic.'[26] A Dáil majority had no right to accept the Treaty and disestablish itself so that it could be reborn as the Provisional Government, which was subservient to London.

Shorn of governmental authority, anti-Treaty politicians like Brugha and de Valera were becoming increasingly irrelevant, losing out to hard-line militarist republicans. In an attempt to reassert himself, de Valera founded Cumann na Poblachta in March, with him at its head, and Brugha as Vice President, but the IRA remained the decisive power bloc. On 22 March, at a press conference held in the offices of de Valera's new political party, Rory O'Connor boasted that he had not even read the Treaty and claimed that 'there are times when revolution was justified and the army had overthrown the government in many countries that way.' When asked if he supported a military dictatorship, he replied 'you can see it that way if you like.'[27] The IRA convention of 26 March formalised the military split. A majority of republican delegates asserted that the IRA was now independent of the Dáil. A 16-man Executive was elected, with Liam Lynch as Chief of Staff. Brugha, seen as a politician, was not on the Executive. A second convention was held on 9 April. It was proposed that the forthcoming election, in which the Treaty was the main issue, should be boycotted. Brugha was opposed to this, as was Liam Lynch, believing that the people had a right to decide for themselves if they accepted the Treaty.

Factions were beginning to emerge within the anti-Treaty side. Lynch sought to find common ground with the provisional government, and de Valera was in talks with Collins about an election pact which might avoid making matters even worse. The more hard-line republicans, such as O'Connor and Liam Mellows, seemed intent on military action. On 14 April, they and their followers occupied several buildings in Dublin city centre and established their HQ in the Four Courts. According to anti-Treaty IRA leader Liam Deasy,

> It appeared as if a number of independent armies were being formed on the anti-Treaty side. Such well known republicans as Rory O'Connor, Seamus Robinson and Liam Mellows could see no good in Michael Collins, Dick Mulcahy and Eoin O'Duffy. This distrust even extended to Liam Lynch, Florrie O'Donoghue, Frank Barrett and myself. We were regarded as being well intentioned but failing to maintain our stand to the Republic.[28]

Lynch, leader of the moderate wing, was excluded from the Four Courts along with his supporters.[29] Brugha was very much on this moderate wing but was powerless to arrest the descent into Civil War. He was distrusted by O'Connor and Mellows because of his association with politics, which is ironic given his later portrayal as a hard-line, militant republican.

The British were becoming increasingly alarmed by the situation. The wording of the new constitution was the last hope of avoiding civil war. It was drafted with the republicans in mind rather than the British with whom the Treaty had been signed. It attempted to heal the Irish fissures by eliminating any role for the Crown. Upon seeing it, Lloyd George informed Collins and Griffith that if they did not amend it they would soon be back at war with the British Army. It was redrafted and was framed within the bounds of the Treaty. It was published on the morning of the election and rejected out of hand by its republican opponents.

The general election that was held on 16 June saw the pro-Treaty Sinn Féin emerging with 239,000 votes compared with 132,161 for anti-Treaty Sinn Féin.[30] Brugha held his seat in Waterford, but this mattered little now. War, at this stage, was inevitable, either with the British or between the Irish themselves. On 18 June, before the results were announced, the republican purists emerged from the Four Courts for a last IRA convention in the Mansion House where they were joined by the less extreme of their ranks, led by Liam Lynch. Tom Barry proposed that the IRA should declare war on the British army in Ireland. His motion was defeated, with Brugha speaking strongly against it.[31] O'Connor and his men returned to their garrison.

CIVIL WAR

The assassination of Sir Henry Wilson on 22 June, the military advisor to the Northern Irish government, brought an ultimatum from London that forced the hand of the provisional government.

On 28 June, Free State forces began shelling the Four Courts. Anti-Treaty leaders, including de Valera and Brugha, met at the Clarence Hotel on the same day and unanimously decided on armed action. They moved behind the anti-Treaty barricades to take up arms against their former comrades. Brugha reported as a private in the Dublin Brigade, his old unit during the Rising. Within two days, the Four Courts had been captured, along with Mellows and O'Connor. The Dublin Brigade, led by Oscar Trayor, held out in the area around O'Connell Street, along with Brugha, de Valera and Ernie O'Malley. Their plan was to keep the Free State army engaged for as long as possible to give the IRA time to slip into the countryside where they had more support. Brugha commanded the IRA rear guard, supported by some members of Cumann na mBan, allowing de Valera and others to escape. According to O'Malley, 'the girls had refused to leave.' They wanted to be treated as equals with the men, and 'the question was debated with heat in rooms of burning buildings, under the noise of shells and the spatter of machine-gun. Cathal Brugha had to exert his personal influence to make them go.'[32] His personal influence notwithstanding, three remained.

The war raged in the North inner city for a week. The buildings around O'Connell Street had been reduced to burning edifices from the Free State bombardment. Emmet Dalton, the Free State Commander, sent a message into Brugha asking him to surrender. Brugha's handwritten reply was sent back in Irish. When Dalton had it translated, he realised it 'read like "'Not dammed likely.'"[33] By 5 July, the building was no longer tenable. Brugha called his small force together and ordered them to give themselves up. As they walked out and handed themselves over to the Free State soldiers, Brugha emerged into a side lane.

There are varying accounts as to the sequences of events and debate over who fired first. Some depict Brugha as heroic or selfless, others as crazed and vengeful, but they all end the same way: he was shot by the Free State soldiers and fell to the ground with blood pouring from his leg. He had carried British shrapnel inside him since the Rising. Added to this now were bullets fired by Irishmen.

Linda Kearns, a nurse who had stayed inside the burning hotel until the last stand, held his severed artery between her fingers while he was driven away.[34] Unconscious in the Mater Hospital, he remained characteristically defiant and obstinate, refusing to die, but lingering for two days, until the end came on 7 July. He was 47 years old, survived by his wife and six children. A note was found in his pocket:

> Why if our last cartridge had been fired, if our last shilling had been spent, and if our last man was lying wounded on the ground, and his English enemies howling round him with their bayonets raised ready to plunge them into his broken body, and if they asked, 'Now, will you come into our Empire?' true to the tradition that has been handed down to him, his answer would be 'No, I will not.'[35]

AFTERMATH

Brugha's death marked the end of the Civil War in Dublin. Upon hearing of his demise, Collins wrote to a friend:

> Many would not have forgiven – had they been in my place – Cathal Brugha's attack on me on January 7th [during the Treaty debates]. Yet I would forgive him anything. Because of his sincerity I would forgive him anything. At worst he was a fanatic – though in what has been a noble cause. At best I number him among the very few who have given their all that this country – now torn by civil war – should have its freedom.

When many of us are forgotten, Cathal Brugha will be remembered.[36]

Within two months, Collins, Arthur Griffith and Harry Boland were dead. The Civil War continued, mainly in Munster, where it became vicious and bitter and infused Irish politics and collective memory for decades to come. The Free State executed 77 IRA prisoners over the course of the war, including the former leaders of the Four Court garrison, Rory O'Connor and Liam Mellows. Liam Lynch was shot on a Tipperary hillside; he died later that day. He was replaced by Frank Aiken as Chief of Staff. On 24 May 1923, he ordered the IRA to 'dump arms', rather than surrender, effectively ending the Civil War.

W. T. Cosgrave, who served under Brugha's command in the South Dublin Union, became President of the Executive Council (head of government), from after Collins' death until 1932. The former Easter rebel successfully and courageously guided the new Free State from its inception through a Civil War and helped to ensure that politics triumphed over violence. He was aided in this by Éamon de Valera. After a few years in the wilderness, he established Fianna Fáil in 1926 and in 1927 took the oath of allegiance to the Crown, leading his 'soldiers of destiny' to take their seats in a parliament that they had refused to recognise five years previous. Fianna Fáil successfully transitioned to power in 1932 and remained there for the next 16 years. De Valera systematically dismantled most parts of the Treaty which he had been opposed to, including the references to the Crown and the oath. He never declared a Republic.

Conclusion

The central argument of this book has been that Brugha was not purely a physical-force advocate. He was convinced that war and politics should be married together in the pursuit of independence. After the Rising, Brugha regarded the IRB as redundant. With the successes of Sinn Féin, Dáil Éireann and the IRA, the secret society was no longer needed. He became implacably opposed to the Brotherhood, believing that it could only pose a danger to political institutions composed of elected representatives. He was centrally involved in the inaugural meeting of the First Dáil and was a minister in the first two governments. During the early months of the War of Independence, Brugha censured IRA offensive actions against the police and army until it became clear that world leaders at the Paris Peace Conference were not prepared to recognise the Irish Republic. He was more concerned with international political opinion than localised attacks on British authorities until it was clear that such action was their only recourse. Throughout the War of Independence, he strove to subordinate the IRA to the Dáil and establish an orthodox relationship between the two. Brugha was innately political and was convinced of the merits and effectiveness of politics. However, given that the British government was not prepared to accept the legitimacy of Irish electoral demands, Irish separatists were forced to fight for independence.

BRUGHA S CHARACTER AND CAREER

Brugha was endowed with a deep-seated intransigence. He did not believe in surrender, and he was always prepared to fight rather than be captured. Forged in the cauldron of the South Dublin Union in 1916, he was cut from the same cloth as that garrison's commander, Éamonn Ceannt. In a final statement, Ceannt regretted the way things had turned out, and he urged republicans 'never to treat with the enemy, never to surrender at his mercy, but to fight to a finish'.[1] These words resonated through the rest of Brugha's life. He had a cavalier disregard for his personal safety, ultimately illustrated by his death in the Civil War.[2]

Those who knew Brugha remarked on his steadfast determination and his resolute commitment to the Republic. Ultimately, however, he was not an unreconstructed republican. He was prepared to accept de Valera's constitutional compromise embodied in Document No 2,[3] and he spoke in favour of external association.[4] This was the biggest compromise of his life, on the biggest issue of its time. The 'metaphysical Republicans' Rory O'Connor and Liam Mellows shouted him down for such moderation[5], with O'Connor eventually admitting that he had not even read the Treaty.[6] In the end, Brugha was not incapable of compromise.

As Minister for Defence, Brugha was, nominally at least, in charge of the army. The fact that the IRA brought the British government to the negotiating table means that his ministerial career must be considered a success. However, there were no Napoleonic plans emanating from the Department of Defence, or indeed GHQ, for much of the war. Local commanders, acting on their own initiative, and often without reference to GHQ or Brugha's department, were *the* decisive military actors in the war. It was their actions, rather than Brugha's skills as a planner, organiser or strategist, which delivered settlement talks in 1921.

In the early stages of the war, Brugha favoured a cautious, defensive policy. Following the suppression of the Dáil in September 1919 and as the prospects of Irish salvation at Paris dwindled, Brugha slowly acquiesced in a more active, confrontational IRA campaign. Throughout the war, he remained deeply uncomfortable at the prospect of civilian causalities: he was reluctant to allow attacks on intelligence personnel; he removed 15 names from the Bloody Sunday hit list as he did not believe there was sufficient evidence against them; he would not allow the execution of women spies.[7] At the same time, he planned to assassinate the British government as they sat in Westminster. He believed that the British cabinet were the ultimate arbiters of political violence in Ireland. He has been portrayed as a one-dimensional gunman, a believer in physical force above all else. This book has attempted to demonstrate that Brugha had complex attitudes to violence. He had brooded over the use of force and had a clear personal belief in the difference between legitimate and illegitimate targets.

Due to the lack of evidence, it is difficult to estimate Brugha's impact on politics between 1919 and 1921. The accusation of Béaslaí and Mulcahy that he was 'hopelessly out of touch'[8] and that he did no useful work[9], must be considered when weighting up judgement on Brugha's political career. So too, must the opinions of Sceilg and Séan MacKeon. MacKeon considered him diligent and competent,[10] while Sceilg dismisses the accusation that Brugha was often absent when he was needed.[11] The reason so little documentary evidence exists is because he almost always reported to the Dáil or cabinet orally. De Valera, writing in 1923 to Brugha's bereaved wife, asserted that '[Brugha's] most important work was scarcely known at all, that is, the work he did at cabinet meetings . . .'.[12] According to Secilg, 'there was no report so enthusiastically endorsed as Cathal Brugha's.'[13] The lack of a paper trail does not necessarily mean that Brugha was a neglectful minister. In fact, in the small amounts of correspondence that have survived, Brugha's replies are prompt and comprehensive.[14]

Brugha's political career can also be considered a success. His central role in the first meeting of Dáil Éireann confers great historical significance upon him. His place at the cabinet table between 1919 and the Treaty split reflects the major contribution he made to Ireland's struggle for independence. His persistent attempts to bring the IRA under the authority of the Dáil were provisionally successful, but were ultimately sundered by the Treaty – which sundered all else before it.

THE LEGACY OF CATHAL BRUGHA

Brugha has become a totem for violent republicanism. His gung-ho exploits in the Rising and his death in the Civil War appeal to the physical-force strain of Irish republicanism, and the London missions, especially his personal involvement during the conscription crisis, compound this. However, it is a fallacy to view Brugha through these few, dramatic, violent snapshots. While his revolutionary career was bracketed by violence – his near-death experience in the South Dublin Union and then his actual death after his defiant last stand at the Hammam Hotel – the interim is punctuated by politics as much as it is by war. In a vacuum of fluid power and violent politics, he endeavoured to lay down a solid democratic relationship between the army and the government. In the fall out over the Treaty, while a bombastic Rory O'Connor was alluding to military dictatorship, Brugha was assuring the Dáil that the army would remain loyal to it.[15] Ultimately, however, he could not deliver this.

Historians have ignored Brugha's inherent belief in politics. When he is viewed through the violent vignettes of 1916 and 1922, it is easy to place him alongside the 'metaphysical' republicans like

O'Connor. It is instructive that O'Connor and his allies regarded Brugha with suspicion because of his association with politics. During the spring and summer of 1922, Brugha had been powerless to affect events because he was perceived as a moderate and a politician by many in the anti-Treaty IRA. He only became relevant in anti-Treaty dynamics once he had a gun in his hand. If Brugha was the one dimensional, gun-toting republican purist as which he has heretofore been presented, he would have been in the Four Courts from mid-April, and most probably in command.

The simplistic analysis which Brugha has been subjected to is symptomatic of the narrow intellectual framework through which historians have addressed the Irish revolution. It is spurious to construct a dichotomy of 'soldiers' and 'politicians.' Violence and politics are not mutually exclusive. Historians have employed these labels as cognitive heuristics, but this approach underestimates the complexities of human attitudes to war and violence, as well as the nebulous dynamics of revolution.

Cathal Brugha's central participation in the first Dáil and his efforts to bring the IRA under the authority of the legislature sit uncomfortably alongside the one-dimensional portrait of him in the existing historiography. It is hoped that this research has gone some way towards rehabilitating the image of Brugha and illuminating his commitment to, and belief in, politics.

Notes

Introduction

1 Sceilg, *Cathal Brugha le Seán MaCealaigh* (Dublin, 1942); Tomás Ó Dochartaigh, *Cathal Brugha: A Shaol is a Thréithe* (Cathair na Mart, 1969).

2 Sceilg, *A Trinity of Martyrs: Terence MacSwiney, Cathal Brugha, Austin Stack* (Dublin, 1947).

3 Diarmaid Ferriter, *A Nation and Not a Rabble: The Irish Revolution 1913–1923* (London, 2015).

4 Roy Foster, *Vivid Faces: The Revolutionary Generation in Ireland 1890–1923* (London, 2014).

5 See, for example, Róisín Ni Ghairbhí, *16 Lives: Willie Pearse* (Dublin, 2015).

6 Michael Laffan, *The Resurrection of Ireland: The Sinn Féin Party, 1916–1923* (Cambridge, 1999), p. 138.

7 Charles Townshend, *The Republic: The Fight for Irish Independence, 1918–1923* (London, 2014), p. 410.

8 Michael Hopkinson, *The Irish War of Independence* (Dublin, 2004), p. 19.

9 Ronan Fanning, *Éamon de Valera: A Will to Power* (London, 2015), pp 126–7.

10 Document No. 2 proposed that Ireland would 'associate' with the Commonwealth in matters such as defence and the monarch would be recognised as the head of this association. There would be no oath of allegiance. For more information, see Chapter Eight.

11 See Chapter Eight.

12 John M Regan, *Myth and the Irish State* (Dublin, 2014), pp 113–21. Regan specifically points to Collins' reluctance to allow the Third Dáil to meet, and his role as Commander and Chief while he was simultaneously president of the IRB.

Chapter One

1   Sceilg quoted in Micheal Ó Cillin, 'Cathal Brugha 1874–1922', in Dublin Historical Record, 38:4 (Sept. 1985).

2   Ibid.

3   Tomás Ó Dochartaigh, *Cathal Brugha: A Shaol is a Thréithe* (Cathair na Mart, 1969), p. 25.

4   Ibid.

5   Ó Cillin, 'Cathal Brugha 1874–1922'.

6   Ó Dochartaigh, *Cathal Brugha*, p. 32.

7   *Freeman's Journal*, 17 June 1912, p. 2.

8   Irish Military Archives, Bureau of Military History, Witness Statement (hereafter, IMA, BMH, WS) 1770, Kevin O'Sheil, pp 208–10.

9   F. X. Martin, 'Introduction', in *The Howth Gun-Running and the Kilcoole Gun-Running* (ed.) F. X. Martin (Dublin, 1963), p. xii.

10   Ibid.

11   Ronan Fanning, *Fatal Path: British Government and Irish Revolution: 1910–1922* (London, 2013), p. 51.

12   Martin, 'Introduction', in *Howth Gun-Running*, p. xii.

13   Diarmaid Ferriter, *The Transformation of Ireland: 1900–2000* (London, 2005), p. 119.

14   Fanning, *Fatal Path*, p. 2.

15   *Irish Freedom*, Apr. 1912, p. 2 quoted in *Winding the Clock: O'Rahilly and the 1916 Rising* (Dublin, 1991), p. 83.

16   'Irish Freedom', June 1912, in ibid., p. 84.

17   F. X. Martin, 'MacNeill and the Irish Volunteers', in *The Scholar Revolutionary: Eoin MacNeill, 1867–1945, and the Making of the New Ireland*, (eds) F. X. Martin and F. J. Byrne (Shannon, 1973), p. 109.

18   *An Claidheamh Soluis*, Nov. 1, 1913.

19   Martin, 'MacNeill and the Irish Volunteers', in *Scholar Revolutionary*, p. 149.

20   James Quinn, 'Brugha, Cathal', in *Dictionary of Irish Biography*, (eds) James McGuire and James Quinn (Cambridge, 2009).

21   Bulmer Hobson, 'The plan succeeds', in *Howth Gun-Running*, pp 128–38.

22   Ibid, p. 129.

23   Ibid, p. 130.

24   Ibid, p. 131.

25   Ibid.

26 Martin, 'Introduction', in *Howth Gun-Running*, p. xvii.

27 Mary Spring Rice, 'Diary of the Asgard', in ibid, p. 95.

28 IMA, BMH, WS 174, James Kenny, p. 2.

29 Diarmaid Ferriter, *A Nation and Not a Rabble: The Irish Revolution 1913–1923* (London, 2014), pp 143–4.

30 IMA, BMH, WS 765, James A. Gubbins, p. 13.

31 Ibid, p. 15.

32 Ibid., 175, John J. Styles, pp 4–5.

33 Mary Gallagher, *16 Lives: Éamonn Ceannt* (Dublin, 2014), p. 204.

34 IMA, BMH, WS 590, Thomas Treacy, pp 8–9.

35 Charles Townshend, 'Making sense of Easter 1916', in *History Ireland* 14:2 (2006), accessed 9 Jan. 2018.

36 IMA, BMH, WS 264, Áine Ceannt, p. 264.

37 Ibid., 174, James Kenny, p. 4.

38 Paul O'Brien, *Uncommon Valour: 1916 and the Battle for the South Dublin Union* (Dublin, 2010), p. 20.

39 Charles Townshend, *Easter 1916: The Irish Rebellion* (London, 2005), p. 173.

40 O'Brien, *Uncommon Valour*, p. 43.

41 IMA, BMH, WS 305, James Coughlan, p. 15.

42 Major Vane in O'Brien, *Uncommon Valour*, p. 76.

43 O'Brien, *Uncommon Valour*, p. 84.

44 IMA, BMH, WS 199, Joseph Doolan, Part 2–3.

45 Ibid.

46 Ibid., Part 2, 4.

47 http://letters1916.maynoothuniversity.ie/diyhistory/scripto/transcribe/1030/2662, accessed 9 Jan. 2018.

Chapter Two

1 Irish Military Archives (hereafter, IMA), Military Service Pension Collection (hereafter, MSPC), Douglas French Mullen, file 20,612 contains an account of Brugha's early efforts to reorganise the Volunteers from his hospital bed.

2 IMA, Bureau of Military Archives, Witness Statement (hereafter, BMH, WS) 601 Henry S. Murray, p. 3.

3 Brian P. Murphy, 'Brugha, Cathal', in *Oxford Dictionary of National Biography* (Oxford, 2004).

4 IMA, BMH, WS 400, Richard Walsh, p. 162.

5   Leon Ó Bríon, *Revolutionary Underground: The Story of the Irish Republican Brotherhood, 1858–1924* (Dublin, 1976), p. 179.

6   Ibid.

7   IMA, BMH, WS 1022, Seán Matthews, pp 6–7.

8   Ibid., WS 392, Éamon T. Dore, p. 8.

9   For example, see ibid., WS 384, Sceilg; ibid., WS 1022, Seán Matthews; ibid., WS 353, James McGuill.

10 Ibid., WS 150, Gregory Murphy, p. 8.

11 R. F. Foster, *Vivid Faces: The Revolutionary Generation in Ireland, 1890–1923* (New York, 2015), p. 261.

12 Michael Laffan, *The Resurrection of Ireland: The Sinn Féin Party, 1916–1923* (Cambridge, 1999), p. 72.

13 Ibid., p. 86.

14 IMA, BMH, WS 400, Richard Walsh, p. 300.

15 *Irish Independent* (hereafter, *II*), 22 May 1917, p. 3.

16 In *Capuchin Annual* (1967), pp 382–3.

17 Diarmaid Ferriter, *A Nation and Not a Rabble: The Irish Revolution 1913–1923* (London, 2014), p. 173.

18 See, for example, *II*, 22 May 1917, p. 3; *II*, 24 Sept. 191,7 p. 3; *II*, 26 Oct. 1917, p. 4.

19 IMA, BMH, WS 264, Áine Ceannt, p. 49. For Lily O'Brennan's own account see IMA, MSPC, File no. 2,229, p. 2.

20 *II*, 19 June 1917, p. 3; *Ulster Herald*, 23 June 1917, p. 4.

21 *II*, 24 Sept. 1917, p. 3.

22 Laffan, *The Resurrection of Ireland*, pp 118–19.

23 IMA, BMH, WS 1766, William O'Brien, 137; also in Laffan, *The Resurrection of Ireland*.

24 IMA, BMH, WS 400, Richard Walsh, p. 150; ibid., 388, Joe Good, p. 39.

25 National Library of Ireland, IR 94109. p. 65.

26 *II*, 26 Oct. 1917, p. 4.

27 *Freeman's Journal*, 27 Oct. 1917, p. 5.

28 Laffan, *The Resurrection of Ireland*, p. 121.

29 Authors who refer to Brugha as Chief of Staff in the period include Ernie O'Malley, in *On Another Man's Wound* (Blackrock, 2002); Piaras Béaslaí, *Michael Collins and the Making of a New Ireland*, Vol. 1 (Dublin, 1926), p. 175. An authoritative article by Florence O'Donoghue does not mention a Chief of Staff, but refers to Brugha as President of the Resident Executive: Florence O'Donoghue, 'Re-organisation of the Irish Volunteers: 1916–1917', in *The Capuchin Annual*, pp 380–5.

30 Richard Mulcahy, 'The Irish Volunteer Convention 27 Oct., 1917', in *The Capuchin Annual*, pp 400–10.

31 Maryann Valiulis, *Portrait of a Revolutionary: General Richard Mulcahy and the Founding of the Irish Free State* (Blackrock, 1992), p. 25.

32 Foster, *Vivid Faces*, p. 263.

33 Diarmaid Ferriter, *The Transformation of Ireland: 1900–2000* (London, 2005), pp 180–1.

Chapter Three

1 Richard Mulcahy, *The Capuchin Annual* (1967), pp 408–9.

2 Maryann Valiulis, *Portrait of a Revolutionary: General Richard Mulcahy and the Founding of the Irish Free State* (Blackrock, 1992), p. 28.

3 Irish Military Archives, Bureau of Military Archives, Witness Statement (hereafter, IMA, BMH, WS) 400, Richard Walsh, pp 39–40.

4 Ibid., WS 369, William Whelan, p. 6.

5 Ibid., WS 1447, John Gaynor, p. 3.

6 Ibid., p. 7.

7 Ibid., WS 388, Joseph Good, p. 43.

8 Ibid., WS 369, William Whelan, p. 65.

9 Ibid., WS 384, Sceilg, p. 40.

10 Tim Pat Coogan, *The IRA* (New York, 1995), p. 95.

11 IMA, BMH, WS 400, Richard Walsh, pp 39–40.

12 Tomás Ó Dochartaigh, *Cathal Brugha: A Shaol is a Thréithe* (Cathair na Mart, 1969), p. 76.

13 *An tÓglach*, 14 Sept. 1918.

14 Ibid., 30 Sept. 1918.

15 IMA, BMH, WS 1479, Seán Healy, p. 52.

16 Pankaj Mishra, *Age of Anger: A History of the Present* (London, 2017), p. 230.

17 University College Dublin Archives, Richard Mulcahy, P7b/190.

Chapter Four

1 James Quinn, 'Brugha, Cathal', in (eds) James McGuire and James Quinn, *Dictionary of Irish Biography* (hereafter, *DOIB*) (Cambridge, 2009).

2 Roy Foster, *Vivid Faces: The Revolutionary Generation in Ireland 1890–1923* (London, 2014), pp 48–50; Brugha's brother, Alfred, also cites the League as an influence on his politics, Irish Military Archives, Bureau of Military Archives, Witness Statement (hereafter, IMA, BMH, WS) 1634, Alfred Burgess, p. 1.

3   See, for example, *Freeman's Journal*, 17 June 1912, p. 2; Piaras Béaslaí, *Michael Collins and the Making of a New Ireland*, Vol. 1 (Dublin, 1926), p. 78.

4   Arthur Mitchell, *Revolutionary Government in Ireland: Dáil Éireann 1919–1922* (Dublin, 1999), p. 17.

5   Béaslaí, *Michael Collins*, Vol. 1, p. 257.

6   Sceilg, *Cathal Brugha le Seán MaCealaigh* (Dublin, 1942), p. 64. This researcher is graciously quoting from a translation provided by Ita Roddy.

7   Sceilg, *Cathal Brugha*, p. 66.

8   Ibid.

9   Ronan Fanning, Michael Kennedy, Dermot Keogh, Eunan O'Halpin (eds), *Documents on Irish Foreign Policy*, Vol. 1: *1919–1922* (Dublin, 1998), pp 1–2, 10–11.

10   Michael Hopkinson, *The Irish War of Independence* (Dublin, 2004), p. 39.

11   Michael Laffan, 'Griffith, Arthur Joseph', in *DOIB*.

12   Tim Pat Coogan, *Michael Collins: A Biography* (London, 1991), p. 231.

13   Darrell Figgis quoted in Mitchell, *Revolutionary Government*, p. 14.

14   Mitchell, *Revolutionary Government*, p. 14.

15   Ronan Fanning, *Éamon de Valera: A Will to Power* (London, 2015), pp 67–8.

16   Coogan, *Michael Collins: A Biography*, p. 102.

17   Collins quoted in Mitchell, *Revolutionary Government*, p. 31.

18   Mitchell, *Revolutionary Government*, p. 32.

19   See, for example, IMA, BMH, WS 400, Richard Walsh, p. 150; IMA, BMH, WS 1770, Kevin O'Sheil, p. 681.

20   Mitchell, *Revolutionary Government*, p. 33.

21   Tom Garvin, *1922: The Birth of Irish Democracy* (Dublin, 1996), p. 56.

22   Maryann Valiulis, *Portrait of a Revolutionary: General Richard Mulcahy and the Founding of the Irish Free State* (Blackrock, 1992), p. 36.

23   James Quinn, 'Brugha, Cathal', in *DOIB*.

24   *Irish Independent* (hereafter *II*), 10 Apr. 1919, p. 7.

25   Charles Townshend, *The Republic: The Fight for Irish Independence 1918-1923* (London, 2014), p. 87.

26   IMA, BMH, WS 400, Richard Walsh, pp 57–8.

27   Quoted in Florence O'Donoghue, *No Other Law: The Story of Liam Lynch and the Irish Republican Army, 1916–1923* (Dublin, 1954), p. 42.

28   Townshend, *The Republic*, p. 86.

29   O'Donoghue, *No Other Law*, p. 43.

30   Diarmuid O'Hegarty quoted in Diarmaid Ferriter, *A Nation and Not a Rabble: The Irish Revolution 1913–1923* (London, 2015), pp 192–3.

31   Valiulis, *Portrait of a Revolutionary*, p. 38.

32   University College Dublin Archives (hereafter, UCDA), Mulcahy, P7b/190.

33 *An tÓglach,* 31 Jan. 1919, p. 1.

34 *An tÓglach*, quoted in Béaslaí, *Michael Collins and the Making*, Vol. 1, p. 275.

35 Béaslaí, *Michael Collins and the Making*, Vol. 1, p. 276.

36 UCDA, Mulcahy, P7b/134.

37 Tomás Ó Dochartaigh, *Cathal Brugha: A Shaol is a Thréithe* (Cathair na Mart, 1969), p. 100.

38 Charles Townshend, 'The IRA and the development of guerrilla warfare', in *English Historical Review*, 94: 371 (1979), pp 318–45.

39 Hopkinson, *War of Independence*, p. 170.

40 Townshend, 'The IRA and the development of guerrilla warfare', pp 318–45.

41 Hopkinson, *War of Independence*, p. 25.

42 UCDA, Éamon de Valera, P150/3618. Brugha to de Valera, 28 Oct 1919. The author would like to thank Donal O'Farrell for translating this letter.

43 IMA, BMH, WS 225, Michael McDonnell, p. 3.

44 O'Donoghue, *No Other Law*, p. 50.

45 IMA, BMH, WS 418, Úna Stack. p. 21.

46 National Archives of the United Kingdom, War Office, 35/95.

47 IMA, BMH, WS 225, Michael McDonnell, p. 4.

48 IMA, BMH, WS 487, Joseph O'Connor, pp 19–20.

49 Coogan, *Michael Collins: A Biography*, p. 143.

Chapter Five

1 Irish Military Archives, Bureau of Military Archives, Witness Statement (hereafter, IMA, BMH, WS) 384, J. J. Sceilg (O'Kelly), p. 50.

2 Arthur Mitchell, *Revolutionary Government in Ireland: Dáil Éireann 1919–1922* (Dublin, 1999), p. 78.

3 IMA, BMH, WS 384 Sceilg, p. 57.

4 Ibid.

5 Ibid., WS 907, Laurence Nugent, p. 223.

6 National Archives of the United Kingdom, War Office (hereafter UKNA, WO), 35/206.

7 IMA, BMH, WS 779, Robert Brenan, p. 22.

8 *Freeman's Journal*, 25 Oct. 1920, p. 6.

9 Maryann Valiulis, *Portrait of a Revolutionary: General Richard Mulcahy and the Founding of the Irish Free State* (Blackrock, 1992), p. 62.

10 Mitchell, *Revolutionary Government*, p. 84.

11 IMA, BMH, WS 907, Joe Nugent, p. 223.

12 Ibid., WS 384, J. J. O'Kelly, pp 56–7.

13 Michael Laffan, *The Resurrection of Ireland: The Sinn Féin Party, 1916–1923* (Cambridge, 1999), p. 32.

14 Mitchell, *Revolutionary Government*, p. 127.

15 IMA, BMH, WS 1479, Seán Healy, p. 46.

16 *Freeman's Journal*, 29 Nov. 1920, pp 4–5.

17 Florence O'Donoghue, *No Other Law: The Story of Liam Lynch and the Irish Republican Army, 1916–1923* (Dublin, 1954), pp 42–3.

18 Charles Townshend, 'The IRA and the development of guerrilla warfare', in *English Historical Review*, 94: 371 (1979), pp 318–45.

19 Mitchell, *Revolutionary Government*, p. 79.

20 IMA, BMH, WS 1479, Seán Healy, p. 52.

21 David Fitzpatrick, 'Boland, Henry James (Harry)', in (eds) James McGuire and James Quinn, *Dictionary of Irish Biography* (Cambridge, 2009).

22 Ibid.

23 University College Dublin Archives (hereafter, UCDA), de Valera, P150/1128.

24 David Fitzpatrick, *Harry Boland's Irish Revolution* (Cork, 2003), p. 182.

25 For a more detailed account of the morning's IRA operation see Anne Dolan, 'Killing and Bloody Sunday: November, 1920', in *The Historical Journal*, 49:3 (2006), pp 789–810.

26 Charles Townshend, *The Republic: The Fight for Irish Independence, 1918–1923* (London, 2014), p. 203.

27 Ernie O'Malley, 'Bloody Sunday', in *Dublin's Fighting Story, 1916–1921: Told by the men who made it*, (ed.) Brian O'Conchubhair (Blackrock, 2009), p. 287.

28 Peter Hart, *Mick: The Real Michael Collins* (London: 2005), p. 241.

29 Quoted in Risteárd Mulcahy, *My Father, The General: Richard Mulcahy and the Military History of the Revolution* (Dublin, 2014), pp 133–4.

30 IMA, BMH, WS 1634, Alfred Burgess, p. 7.

31 For example, Laffan, *The Resurrection of Ireland*, p. 138; Michael Hopkinson, *The Irish War of Independence* (Dublin, 2004), p. 19.

32 The Treaty Debates, 7 Jan. 1922: http://www.ucc.ie/celt/published/E900003-001/, accessed 21 July 2015.

33 Ernie O'Malley, *The Singing Flame* (Dublin, 1978), p. 137.

34 IMA, BMH, WS 199, Joseph Doolan, p. 3.

35 Ibid., WS 1022, Seán Matthews, p. 7.

36 National Library of Ireland, Ceannt, Ms 3198.

37 Mitchell, *Revolutionary Government*, pp 222–3.

38 UCDA, de Valera, P150/1415.

39 Ibid.

40 Ibid.

41 Townshend, *The Republic*, p. 86. Ernest Blythe claimed that the tensions between Brugha and Collins arose earlier, around April 1919. IMA, BMH, WS 939, Ernest Blythe, p. 118.

42 See, for example, IMA, BMH, WS 304, James Coughlan, p. 15.

43 Tomás Ó Dochartaigh, *Cathal Brugha: A Shaol is a Thréithe* (Cathair na Mart, 1969), p. 81.

44 Hart, *The Real Michael Collins*, p. 71.

45 See, for example, Piaras Béaslaí, *Michael Collins and the Making of a New Ireland*, Vol. 1 (Dublin, 1926), pp 78–9 for a positive picture. Ernie O'Malley, *On Another Man's Wound* (Blackrock, 2002), pp 112–3 comments on Brugha's aloofness. Joe Goode and William Whelan were both in London with Brugha in 1918 to assassinate the cabinet. Their radically different impressions of Brugha during this time can be found in their BMH, WS: IMA, BMH, WS 388, Joe Goode, pp 41–8; IMA, BMH, WS 369, William Whelan, pp 5–8.

46 Béaslaí, *Michael Collins*, Vol 1, p. 78.

47 Hopkinson, *War of Independence*, p. 18.

48 UCDA Mulcahy, P7/D/70.

49 Ibid., P7/b/177.

50 Patrick Murray, 'Obsessive Historian', in *Proceedings of the Royal Irish Academy*, 101 C (2001), pp 37–65.

51 J. J. Lee, *Ireland, 1912–1985: Politics and Society* (Cambridge, 1989), p. 47.

52 Hopkinson, *War of Independence*, pp 177–84.

Chapter Six

1 Margery Forester, *Michael Collins: Lost Leader* (London, 1971), p. 192.

2 Irish Military Archives, Bureau of Military Archives, Witness Statement (hereafter, IMA, BMH, WS) 1716, Seán MacKeon, p. 160.

3 Ibid., p. 162.

4 Arthur Mitchell, *Revolutionary Government in Ireland: Dáil Éireann 1919–1922* (Dublin, 1999), p. 216; Michael Hopkinson, *The Irish War of Independence* (Dublin, 2004), p. 88; *Freeman's Journal*, 29 Nov. 1920, p. 3.

5 IMA, BMH, WS 1716, Seán MacKeon, p. 168; Padraic Colum, *Arthur Griffith* (Dublin, 1959), p. 223.

6 IMA, BMH, WS 1716, Seán MacKeon, p. 168.

7 Peter Hart, 'Michael Collins and the assassination of Sir Henry Wilson', in *Irish Historical Studies*, 28:110 Nov. 1992, pp 150–70.

8 Tim Pat Coogan, *Michael Collins: A Biography* (London, 1991), pp 180–1.

9 Mitchell, *Revolutionary Government*, p. 227.

10 University College Dublin Archives (hereafter, UCDA), Éamon de Valera, P150/1128. Brugha to Boland, 2 Mar. 1921.

11 Peter Hart, *I.R.A. at War 1916–1923* (Ocfrod, 2005), p. 181.

12 David Fitzpatrick, *Harry Boland's Irish Revolution* (Cork, 2003), p. 210.

13 UCDA, Éamon de Valera, P150/1128, Boland to Brugha, 30 Mar. 1921.

14 Ibid., 22 Apr. 1921.

15 Ibid., 21 June 1921.

16 Ibid., 2 Mar. 1921.

17 Quoted in Fitzpatrick, *Boland's Irish Revolution*, p. 216.

18 Brugha, quoted in ibid., p. 217.

19 Mitchell, *Revolutionary Government*, p. 79.

20 Collins quoted in Peter Hart, *Mick: The Real Michael Collins* (London: 2005), p. 263.

21 UCDA, Éamon de Valera, P150/1387, Brugha to de Valera, 16 Mar. 1921.

22 For a comprehensive account of the history of the fluctuation to the British Pound, see Robert Twigger, 'Inflation: The value of the Pound 1750–1998' Research Paper 99/20. Economic Policy and Statistics Sect., House of Commons Library (1999).

23 Average exchange rate in 1921 was £1 = $3.85. See: http://www.measuringworth.com/datasets/exchangepound/result.php, accessed, 30 June 2015.

24 Hart, *The Real Michael Collins*, p. 263.

25 Uinseann MacKeon, *Survivors: The Story of Ireland's Struggle to the Present Time* (Dublin, 1987), p. 405.

26 Coogan, *Michael Collins: A Biography*, pp 175–7.

27 Ibid., p. 34.

28 UCDA, Richard Mulcahy, P7b/192, Brugha to Mulcahy, 2 May 1921.

29 Richard Mulcahy quoted in Risteárd Mulcahy, *My Father, The General: Richard Mulcahy and the Military History of the Revolution* (Dublin, 2014), p. 131.

30 UCDA, Éamon de Valera, P150/1387, Brugha to de Valera, 16 Mar. 1921.

31 UCDA, Éamon de Valera, P150/1128, Brugha to Boland, 9 Aug. 1921.

32 Hart, *The Real Michael Collins*, p. 264.

33 Charles Townshend, 'The IRA and the development of guerrilla warfare', in *English Historical Review*, 94: 371 (1979), pp 318–45.

34 Mulcahy quoted in Mulcahy, *My Father, The General*, p. 56. For Brugha's attitude to open warfare, see UCDA, de Valera, P150/3618.

35 Risteárd, *My Father, The General*, pp 56–7.

36 Maryann Valiulis, *Portrait of a Revolutionary: General Richard Mulcahy*

and the Founding of the Irish Free State (Blackrock, 1992), p. 62.

37 UCDA, de Valera, P150/1128, Brugha to Boland, 9 Aug. 1921; UCDA, Ernie O'Malley, P17(a)/158, RO'B to Brugha, 14 Nov. 1921.

38 UCDA, O'Malley, P17(a)/2, MacMahon to Brugha, 19 Dec. 1921; IMA, BMH, WS 935 Seán Harling, p. 7.

39 Charles Townshend, *The Republic: The Fight for Irish Independence, 1918-1923* (London, 2014), p. 315.

Chapter Seven

1 University College Dublin Archives (hereafter, UCDA), Ernie O'Malley, P17a/158, Boland to Brugha, 19 July 1921.

2 Ibid.

3 Charles Townshend, *The Republic: The Fight for Irish Independence, 1918-1923* (London, 2014), p. 326.

4 UCDA, Ernie O'Malley, P17(a), Department of Quarter Master General to Ministry of Defence 19 Dec. 1921.

5 Ibid., Richard Mulcahy, P7/A/22. Brugha to A/General 30 July 1921.

6 Ibid., Mulcahy to Brugha 2 Sept. 1921.

7 Ibid., Brugha to Mulchay, 6 Sept. 1921.

8 Ibid., 13 Sept. 1921.

9 Townshend, *The Republic*, p. 329.

10 Maryann Valiulis, *Portrait of a Revolutionary: General Richard Mulcahy and the Founding of the Irish Free State* (Blackrock, 1992), p. 105.

11 Ibid., p. 107.

12 Townshend, *The Republic*, p. 326.

13 Ibid., p. 330.

14 Hopkinson, *Green against Green: The Irish Civil War* (Dublin, 2004), p. 25.

15 Frank Pakenham, 'Peace by Ordeal', quoted in J. J. Lee, *Ireland, 1912–1985: Politics and Society* (Cambridge, 1989), p. 50.

16 Máire Comerford quoted in Cal McCarthy, *Cumman na mBan and the Irish Revolution* (Dublin, 2014), p. 256.

17 See, for example, Piaras Béaslaí, *Michael Collins and the Making of a New Ireland*, Vol 2, p. 336; Townshend, *The Republic*, p. 360; Tim Pat Coogan, *Michael Collins: A Biography* (London, 1991), pp 304–6. For contemporary criticism of Brugha's remarks, see UCDA, Sighle Humphreys, P106/727, Jennie Wyse Power to Sighle Humphreys, 8 Jan. 1922.

18 The Treaty Debates: http://www.ucc.ie/celt/published/E900003-001/ accessed 14 June 2015.

19 Ibid.

20 Ibid.

21 Peter Hart, *Mick: The Real Michael Collins* (London: 2005), p. 338.

22 Irish Military Archives, Bureau of Military Archives, Witness Statement (hereafter, IMA, BMH, WS) IMA, BMH, Secilg, pp 384, 30.

23 Diarmaid Ferriter, *A Nation and Not a Rabble: The Irish Revolution 1913–1923* (London, 2015), p. 258.

24 *Irish Independent*, 3 Mar. 1922, p. 3.

25 McCarthy, *Cumman na mBan*, p. 263.

26 See Chapter Six.

27 Michael Hopkinson, 'From truce to Civil War, 1921–2', in *A New History of Ireland VII: Ireland 1921–84*, (ed.) J. R. Hill (Oxford, 2003), p. 18.

28 Liam Deasy, *Brother against Brother* (Cork, 1998), p. 39.

29 Ibid., p. 42.

30 Ferriter, *A Nation*, p. 262.

31 Seán MacBride in Uinseann Mac Eoin, *Survivors*, (Dublin, 1980), p. 129.

32 Ernie O' Malley, *The Singing Flame*, (Dublin, 1978), p. 131.

33 Emmet Dalton papers, National Library of Ireland MS 10,973/11/15, 4 July 1922 Report received from Capt. Dalton, Amiens Street, 10.15pm, 3/7/22.

34 Margret Ward, *Unmanageable Revolutionaries: Women and Irish Nationalism*, (1983, London), p. 185.

35 UCDA, Éamon de Valera, P150/3618.

36 Collins, quoted in Coogan, *Michael Collins: A Biography*, p. 387.

Conclusion

1 National Library of Ireland, Ceannt, Ms 3198.

2 See, for example, Irish Military Archives, Bureau of Military Archives, Witness Statement (hereafter, IMA, BMH, WS), Alfred Burges, p. 7; ibid., 1022, Seán Matthews, p. 7.

3 University College Dublin Archives (hereafter, UCDA), Éamon de Valera, P150/3618.

4 *Irish Independentt* (hereafter, *II*), 20 Feb. 1922. p. 5.

5 J. J. Lee, *Ireland: 1912–1985: Politics and Society* (Cambridge, 1989), p. 51.

6 Michael Laffan, *The Resurrection of Ireland: The Sinn Féin Party, 1916–1923* (Cambridge, 1999), p. 364.

7 Ernie O' Malley, *The Singing Flame*, (Dublin, 1978), p. 137.

8 Béaslaí, *Michael Collins and the making of a New Ireland, Vol I*, p. 99.

9 Risteárd Mulcahy, *My Father, The General: Richard Mulcahy and the Military History of the Revolution* (Dublin, 2014).

10 MacKeon, see above.

11 IMA, BMH, WS 384, Sceilg, pp 56–7.

12 UCDA P150/3618, Éamon de Valera to Kathleen Brugha, 6 Feb. 1923.

13 IMA, BMH, WS 384, Secilg, p. 57.

14 See, for example Brugha's correspondence with Mulcahy regarding the Robbie case: UCDA, Mulcahy, P7/a/1; or Brugha's correspondence with Boland, UCDA P150/1128.

15 Michael Hopkinson, 'From Treaty to Civil War, 1921–2', in *A New History of Ireland VII: Ireland 1921–84*, (ed.) J. R. Hill (Oxford, 2003), p. 11.

Select Bibliography

Primary Sources

Brugha has previously been neglected by historians and biographers because of the lack of sources. He was extremely reticent to commit anything to paper for security reasons. There are no diaries and almost no significant correspondence. There is no collection of Brugha's personal papers, though his first biographer Sceilg states that he had access to such a repository when writing his books. A helpful and knowledgeable family member told this researcher that anything which the family had relating to Brugha has been put into the care of state institutions. In the absence of such material, scholars must turn to the archives of his contemporaries and colleagues for evidence of his life and career. The Mulcahy and de Valera papers are invaluable in this regard. While no source is unimpeachable, the personal papers of politicians who were directly involved in the events covered by this study can pose particular problems. Both Mulcahy and de Valera went on to have long, albeit divergent, political careers following the Revolution. Both have preserved a record which presents themselves and their allies in a favourable light. Mulcahy, in particular, has sought to minimise Brugha's role as Minister, while promoting himself and Collins as the decisive agents in the war. He has also sought to distance himself and Collins from what perhaps came to be seen as the dirtier side of the conflict, particularly the missions to assassinate the British cabinet in the House of Commons.

The more recently released Bureau of Military History Witness Statements (BMH WS) not only add texture and a human quality to the pre-existing archival sources, but they also allow for other recollections and points of view to be incorporated into the history of this period. Mulcahy and de Valera no doubt allowed politics to inform what they preserved in their archives and what they discarded. We should not be so naive as to think that the Witness

Statements are not susceptible by such post-hoc sensibilities. What they do offer, however, are other windows – diverse and often conflicting – through which scholars can view the period. By drawing on new sources such as the BMH and the Military Service Pension Collection (MSPC), revisiting older ones like the Mulcahy and de Valera archives, and augmenting them with other sources like contemporary newspaper reports, this book has sought to revise the portrait of Cathal Brugha.

Secondary literature

Although two Irish-language biographies of Brugha exist, the lack of a dedicated study of Brugha in the English language has contributed to the distorted image of him in the secondary literature. Brugha's friend and political ally J. J. O'Kelly, writing under the penname Sceilg, published the first attempt, *Cathal Brugha,* in 1942. The book is written in the old Irish script, decommissioned in 1963, rendering it esoteric to all but the most initiated. It is typical of the historiography of this period: reverent, hagiographical and overtly nationalist. Chapter two is a 5,000 word tract on Ireland's history from the Norman conquest to Cromwell. The book is nonetheless important as it represents the first attempt to record the details of Brugha's life. In 1947, Sceilg published *A Trinity of Martyrs: Terrence Mac Swiney, Cathal Brugha, Austin Stack.* The Brugha section of the book mainly focuses on the period from the Truce until his death almost exactly a year later. These are character sketches drawn in black and white; Brugha appears in a highly favourable light throughout. Brugha's nephew, Tómás Ó Dochartaigh, published the hagiographical *Cathal Brugha: A Shaol is a Thréithe* (Cathair na Mart, 1969). Also in Irish, it is a shorter though more focused account of Brugha's life and draws on Sceilg's earlier work. Brugha practically disappears from Ó Dochartaigh's narrative in 1920, only to remerge around the time of the Truce. This is symptomatic of the paucity of documentary evidence on Brugha.

Scattered through various publications are short biographical chapters of Brugha. For example, *History's Daughter: A Memoir from the Only Child of Terrence MacSwiney* by Máire MacSwiney Brugha (Dublin, 2005) contains a short Brugha portrait written by his grandson, Cathal Brugha, which is understandably favourable. Risteárd Mulcahy's family memoir, *My Father, the General: Richard Mulcahy and the Military History of the Revolution* (Dublin, 2009) includes a short section on Brugha. The author's primary sources are exclusively Mulcahy sources: his tapes, his personal papers and his lengthy annotations of Piaras Béaslaí's biography of Collins. Brugha is depicted as aloof and brusque, but also not 'much occupied' by military matters or politics until de Valera's return from America at the end of 1920. The book is a useful digest of the Mulcahy papers, but its biases are obvious and understandable. A 1966 lecture delivered by Major Florence O'Donoghue is the best English-language account of Brugha's life and times. It is measured, though plays down the feud with Collins and totally ignores Brugha's audacious plans of political assassination. Michael Ó Cillin read a shorter paper to the Old Dublin Society in 1985, but it offered no new content.

To study Brugha properly, it is first essential to examine the Irish Revolution. Though writing on the period prior to the 1960s was a largely hagiographical affair, some useful books did appear which serve at least to chart the course of events and attitudes towards key individuals. Dorothy MacArdle's *The Irish Republic* (Dublin, 1937) and Piaras Béaslaí's two volume *Michael Collins and the Making of a New Ireland* (Dublin, 1926) offer differing political views on the course of the revolution. Many excellent books have appeared in recent years which are invaluable when situating Brugha within his wider context. Diarmaid Ferriter's *A Nation and Not a Rabble: The Irish Revolution 1913–1923* (London, 2015), Michael Hopkinson's *The Irish War of Independence* (Dublin, 2002) and Charles Townshend's *The Republic: The Fight for Irish Independence, 1918–1923* (London, 2013) are all highly informative and thoroughly researched. Roy Foster's atmospheric *Vivid Faces: The Revolutionary Generation in Ireland 1890–1923* (London, 2014) is also an essential work on the period and it brings many of Brugha's contemporaries to life.

Understanding Brugha's contemporaries is key to understanding Brugha. Michael Hopkinson astutely observed that Michael Collins 'had a surer grasp of the limitations of his achievement than many of his biographers.' Differing perspective on Collins can be found in Tim Pat Coogan's *Michael Collins: A Biography* (London, 1991) and Peter Hart's *Mick: The Real Michael Collins* (London, 2005). There is no definitive book on his life – but can there ever be? The same could be said of de Valera, though he has been more judiciously served by Ronan Fanning. His recent biography *Éamon de Valera: A Will to Power* (London, 2015) is a succinct distillation of the most influential Irishman of the last century. Maryann Gialanella Valiulis' *Portrait of a Revolutionary: General Richard Mulcahy and the Founding of the Irish Free State* (Dublin, 1992) is an absorbing and balanced biography. Mary Gallagher, *16 Lives: Éamonn Ceannt* (Dublin, 2014), Dave Hannigan *Terrence MacSwiney: The Hunger Strike that Rocked an Empire* (Dublin, 2010) and Florence O'Donoghue *No Other Law: The Story of Liam Lynch and the Irish Republican Army* (Dublin, 1954) are all useful on Brugha's fellow travellers. The best work on the Irish Revolution by those who shaped in can be found in C. S. Andrews' *Dublin Made Me* (Dublin, 1979) and Ernie O'Malley's *On Another Man's Wound* (London, 1936) and *The Singing Flame* (Dublin, 1978).

There are many specialist studies on more niche aspects of the period. For political considerations, see Arthur Mitchell *Revolutionary Government in Ireland: Dáil Éireann 1919–22* (Dublin, 1995) and Michael Laffan *The Resurrection of Ireland: The Sinn Féin Party, 1916–1923* (Cambridge, 1999). For the surreptitious operations of the IRA and its secretive antecedences, see T. Ryle Dwyre *The Squad and the Intelligence Operations of Michael Collins* (Cork, 2005) and Leon O'Brion *Revolutionary Underground: The Story of the Irish Republican Brotherhood, 1958–1924* (Dublin, 1976). Brugha was in combat twice; both were significant events in his own life and the course of the Revolution. They are done justice by Paul O'Brien's *Uncommon Valour: 1916 and the Battle for the South Dublin Union* (Cork, 2010) and Liz Gillis *The Fall of Dublin: 28 June to 5 July 1922* (Cork 2011). Michael Hopkinson's *Green against Green: The Irish Civil War* (Dublin, 2004) remains unsurpassed as the best history of the fratricidal conflict, while his article in *A New History of Ireland VII* (Oxford, 2003), 'From Treaty to Civil War:1921–2', neatly bridges the divide between his two longer works. *Easter 1916: The Irish Rebellion* (London, 2005) by Charles Townshend is an indispensable account of the Rising.

Index